The Naked Trader's Guide to Spread Betting

Also by Robbie Burns

The Naked Trader:
How anyone can make money trading shares (2nd edition)

www.nakedtrader.co.uk

The
Naked Trader's
Guide to
Spread Betting

How to make money from shares in up or down
markets

by Robbie Burns

Hh

HARRIMAN HOUSE LTD

3A Penns Road
Petersfield
Hampshire
GU32 2EW
GREAT BRITAIN

Tel: +44 (0)1730 233870
Fax: +44 (0)1730 233880
Email: enquiries@harriman-house.com
Website: www.harriman-house.com

First published in Great Britain in 2010
Reprinted 2012 and 2013

Author photos by Jim Marks
Cartoons by Peter Dredge and Roy Mitchell
Charts copyright © ShareScope
Other images copyright © iStock International Inc.

Set in Plantin, Clarendon and Eurostile

ISBN: 978-1-906659-23-3

British Library Cataloguing in Publication Data
A CIP catalogue record for this book can be obtained from the British Library.

Printed and bound in the UK by CPI Group (UK) Ltd, Croydon, CR0 4YY.

Contents

About the Author

After starting work as a reporter and editor for various local newspapers, Robbie worked as editor of ITV and Channel 4's teletext services. He also wrote ITV's daily teletext soap opera 'Park Avenue' for 5 years. He then went on to freelance for various newspapers, including *The Independent* and *The Sun*, and also helped set up a financial news service for CNN. In 1997 he became editor of BSkyB's teletext services and set up their shares and finance service. While there he also set up various entertainment phone lines in conjunction with BSkyB, including a *Buffy the Vampire Slayer* phone line.

He left full-time work in 2001 to trade and run his own businesses, which included a café in London that he later sold, doubling his money on the initial purchase.

While at BSkyB, Robbie broadcast a diary of his share trades, which became hugely popular. He transferred the diary to his website, www.nakedtrader.co.uk, which became one of the most-read financial websites in the UK. Between 2002 and 2005 he wrote a column for *The Sunday Times*, 'My DIY Pension', featuring share buys and sells made for his pension fund, which he runs himself in a SIPP (self-invested personal pension). As chronicled in these articles, he managed to double the money in his pension fund from £40,000 to £80,000 in less than three years. By 2009 he had doubled it again, reaching £165,000. Robbie now writes a weekly column for the leading financial website, ADVFN.com.

Robbie has made a tax-free profit of nearly £800,000 since 1999, as chronicled in his twice-weekly website updates, and has made a profit every year, even during the market downturns of 2000-2002 and 2008-2009.

He lives in a riverside apartment on the Thames in London with his wife, Elizabeth, son Christopher and cat Domino. His hobbies include chess, running, swimming, horse racing, listening to rubbish dance music and trading shares from his bedroom, erm ... naked. After all, he wouldn't be seen dead in a thong ... (though he has been seen in Speedos).

Welcome to the World of Spread Betting

Why *did I write this book?* For the money? You've gotta be kidding. If you want to get rich, don't write finance books.

I get a lot of emails asking about spread betting, so I took a look at the books that were available and there seemed to be a gap in the market for a beginner's book that wasn't either too complicated or too dull.

Funnily enough, in order to succeed at spread betting you don't actually *have* to be confused and bored all the time! So I decided to write that missing book – a helpful and complete guide that you can dip into and out of, and enjoy without having to scratch your head every other page.

Another reason for writing it is that I believe many new spread bettors are not fully aware of the risks involved and how careful you have to be. This book contains some horror stories – but I hope, because you are reading it, that you won't end up as another one of those stories. It's a fact that more people lose than win at spread betting. A lot more. This book is designed to get you on the right foot and make you one of the few winners.

And so I trust with this book you'll not have to give up on it after a few pages because it's too hard to read and full of jargon, and that it'll put you on the path to some happy and stress-free spread betting adventures. A decent, easy-read guide to spread betting has been needed for some time: one written by someone who has actually spread bet for a few years and can cut through all the nonsense, rather than a journalist wanting to make a few extra quid. I have done all I can to make this that book.

It's All About Me – and You

The Naked Trader and spread betting

This book is designed to be read with my other book, *The Naked Trader*. If you're in a bookshop right now, you should be able to find a copy nearby!

The reason for this is not because I want to sell two books instead of one* (you cynic!) but because *The Naked Trader* deals with all aspects

of share trading from the beginning, such as how to get share quotes, understand company statements and valuations, my strategies, etc – all of which can be used in your spread betting. This book builds on, rather than repeats, such fundamental advice (which is better value when you think about it).

So this book expects you to have read *The Naked Trader* first! It assumes that you have probably already done some kind of investing or trading in shares, and you know how to buy a share online, but you now want to go further and start spread betting.

Who this book is for

This book is a beginner's guide to spread betting – how to do it, and some ideas and techniques on how to make money from doing it well (or at least on how to not lose too much). Indeed, we will look a lot at how you have to be careful – there are many pitfalls with spread betting.

It's especially for you if you've already traded shares from time to time in the normal way, but have heard about spread betting and are wondering whether it's something you could (or should) be doing. It isn't for you if you've been doing it for years and know all about it. Nor

---

* Believe me, selling you two instead of one doesn't even get me a cup of coffee at Starbucks.

is it for you if you're looking for technical analysis or strategies involving charts, lines and divergences – there are plenty of other books for you on those topics!

So the book is for you at the *start* of your spread betting journey. If you're sitting there already happily spread betting away, then you probably need to read a more advanced book. But if you've heard about spread betting, thought about it but got too scared to do it, then this book may help. It'll also help if you're a straightforward investor fed up with losing money from markets tanking: here you'll learn how to make money easily from shares going *down*.

Lastly, maybe you've never looked at the markets before, but are intrigued about doing it via spread betting. Well, certainly as part of a broader investing strategy, I think spread betting can be good. And this book will help you, too.

What this book ISN'T about is *very* short-term trading, or how to trade volatile instruments like oil and commodities. For that type of thing you need to look for a different book.

Spread betting

I've given up mentioning spread betting at parties or social gatherings. The moment you say 'spread betting' you've lost the person you're talking to. Their eyes glaze over and immediately you're marked as some kind of boring weirdo. Now I just pretend I own a boarding home for cats, which always seems more fascinating to people I meet. (Though I did have a terrible evening talking to someone who *really did* want to run a cats' home. I had to spend the whole evening inventing stories about it.)

Yet little do they know how fantastic spread betting can be. Far from being boring, it's one of the most exciting tools out there for investors and traders. In fact, it's actually a tool with so many advantages that I think it's crazy that people either ignore it, or, even worse, think it's too complicated (it's actually extremely simple).

For example, without spread betting it would have been hard to make money out of the big FTSE fall in 2008. As you can see from the chart, the FTSE fell for a long time and some spread bet shorts in this year helped me to make some money.

Epic FTSE fall

So, really, that is what this book is all about: explaining how simple it all is, and helping you avoid the pitfalls that are involved.

All about me...

Yes, my name really is Robbie Burns. No, not Scottish. No good at poetry either. Come to think of it, not much good at anything except eating chocolate.

Let me tell you a bit about me. After all, there really is nothing like talking about yourself, is there?

You might think as a trader that I'm some kind of banker (I said "banker"!) in a pinstriped suit and tie... or maybe some kind of wide boy... No. Definitely not the suit. You're more likely to find me in a pair of pyjama bottoms and a t-shirt. Just ask the Tesco delivery guy. Or Waitrose if I'm feeling flush.

You might think I'm like one of those posh blokes you see on the telly, giving their financial forecasts. Wrong again. You also might think I know a lot about economics, commodity pricing, the macro economy and the rest of it. Wrong again! My economic knowledge is limited. And for some reason people think I'm a cockney. No!

Maybe I was a maths genius at school ... No. Did I get amazing qualifications? No! Was I left a whole pile of money to trade with? Not at all. I never got left a bean.

None of this matters! I can still trade the markets and make money.

I haven't had a job since 2001. Yippee! I've not had to put on a tie, no tedious journey to the same horrible office every day, no office politics, no fear of redundancy.

I'm not especially good at maths. I've got a low concentration threshold (... umm, what was I doing? Oh yes, writing a book), and am a bit impatient. But it doesn't matter; I have still made a fortune from the markets. It does take some common sense and some understanding of your own brain and psychological makeup. Not much else, though.

Spread betting has long been a valuable part of my market armoury, and it especially helped me to make money during the bear markets (down markets) of 2000-2002 and 2008-2009. But the main thing is that over the years I've used it (and other techniques) to make constant money on the market *whether down or up*, as catalogued twice a week at my website www.nakedtrader.co.uk.

I've been spread betting since 2000. Am I that old now? Never mind, with age comes maturity.

The money from spread betting has been very handy, helping me with house deposits and that kind of thing. I'm more likely to actually use the profits from spread betting than the money I've built up in ISAs.

Admittedly I had a lucky start: when I began trading, the markets were booming and, like everyone else, I bought lots of silly internet stocks that were going through the roof. As history now reveals, of course, it was a massive bubble. But exciting days. A stock could be 50p, then announce it had set up an internet site and in seconds it was 150! If it was tipped by the geezers in the *Daily Mirror* at the time, it could double overnight. Its actual quality didn't much matter.

I was also lucky in that I sold all the rubbish tech stocks I had spread bet on near the top.

For example, I spread bet a company called Scoot – can't even remember what it was supposed to do, something to do with mobiles, I think. Bought at 50p and sold at 320. Lovely!

Then came the downturn, and that's when spread betting really came into its own for me, and I used it to bet on shares to go down. The profits from downbets, also known as 'shorts', for some reason were more rewarding than the upbets.

Since then I've used spread betting constantly, together with my normal share trading.

And you know what? Surprisingly, I'm bored of talking about myself now, so...

What about you?

You're not one of those people who buys a financial book, reads a couple of pages, then puts it on the bookshelf thinking one day you might look at it again, are you? Hey, that's fine by me, I still get my half a cup of Starbucks whether you read one page or the whole lot.

But I would hope you're someone who really is set on getting the most out of this experience. Maybe you want to start branching out with your investing; perhaps you want to make some money when markets fall; or maybe you just to want to make some useful money on the side.

Or maybe you want to be able to, one day, like me, use spread betting to help you make a living – and leave that commute behind.

All this is possible! But though it's possible it's not necessarily easy.

Anyone can do it but...

To be a winner you must have discipline and self-will. I believe we all possess the means to do it, but those who start gambling, overtrading or ignore all the warnings I give in this book will fall by the wayside and lose money.

However, the beauty of spread betting, trading or investing is that it's a great leveller, because as long as you have some money you can afford to lose, you can do it. You don't have to be some pinstriped City type.

It doesn't matter whether you consider yourself to be working class, middle class, upper class or even the Queen. You could be a plumber, dentist, fireman, housewife, unemployed, nanny; it doesn't matter a bean. You can make money using spread betting as a key part of an investment armoury.

However ... do be warned! While I have little doubt that anyone with the right discipline can make money spread betting, more people lose at it than win. And that's a fact. If you want to make money, you need to understand what you're doing and have a plan. If you don't, you'll lose.

The winners, in my opinion, are winners because they have a plan. The losers either don't have the right temperament for it, overdo it, start gambling, or commit a lot of other mistakes which we'll discuss later in the book.

If you lose consistently at spread betting, you must quickly consider if you are just not suited for it and, if that's the case, give it up. There is little point throwing good money after bad. So now...

Shall we get started?

(I suppose now I've started this book, like in *Mastermind*, I've got to finish it. Sometime this century. The publisher's been waiting long enough.)

So ... spread betting, eh?

You little devil! Thinking of giving it a bash by buying this book.

Okay, well, I hope you've come to the right place. Let's get things straight between us right from the start.

I PROMISE:

- to tell you all about spread betting,

- without using fancy words, or jargon,

- and without boring the knickers off you (hopefully).

YOU PROMISE:

- to try to read the whole thing, and not skip too much,

- not to smear the book with jam or beer. I just won't have it and will be round your house if I find out, and

- not to take the book to bed (it could ruin your love life).

Got that? Right.

Are you sitting comfortably? Then let's begin. (If you're not sitting comfortably there are some rather good creams around – piles of them.)

Robbie
London, 2010

PART I:
LEARNING IT

1. Before We Get to the Detail

The nature of spread betting

There is one thing above all that you must understand before you start spread betting and that is:

 You are not investing by buying real shares in a market. You are BETTING, and you are betting with what, in effect, is a bookmaker!

When you buy or sell anything with a spread betting company YOU DON'T OWN A SINGLE SHARE. You are betting on whether a share price is going to go up or down. And it is so easy. With one click you can be making, or losing, money.

Generally speaking, unlike, say, a normal bookie – which takes your bets on the horses and makes money from you losing – the really good thing about spread betting companies is:

They won't shut you down if you win.

If you start winning a lot on the horses, for example, you'll probably find your account shut down because you are costing the bookie money. But with a financial spread bet, the bookie still makes money off you even if you win a lot! You can win millions and they won't bat an eyelid.

That's because, unlike a normal bookie, it is not necessarily you versus the spread betting firm. The 'bookie' in this case can easily earn money from every trade you make, whether it's a winner or a loser (more on how later) and so the spread-bet firm just wants you to trade.

And best of all – there is no tax to pay!

If you make a mint you can keep it! No sleazy politician can get his or her paws on your winnings. Although, of course, like those irritating ads say, tax laws can change, and it's possible they could tax spread betting in the future. But they don't at the moment, so enjoy.

Spread betting as part of an overall strategy

I do think spread betting should be considered as part of an overall investment strategy, so think twice about only spread betting and nothing else. It should, I think, be seen as an add-on to other investments or trading. For example, if, like me, you have a decent share portfolio but the market goes down for a couple of weeks, you could use spread betting to make money from the short-term downside while keeping your portfolio intact.

> Think of spread betting as a starter, or very tasty side dish, but not necessarily the main course.

So what have we got so far then – have you been paying attention? Just a reminder:

- you are placing bets with the equivalent of a bookie,
- you don't own the shares you bought or sold, and
- you can make as much as you like tax-free.

Before We Go Any Further: a Warning

Are you the right sort of person to spread bet?

Without wanting to sound old fartish about this… [You old fart! – Ed] Remember I just said the spread firms would like you to trade a lot because then they make more money? Good. Well, of course, most spread betting sites are geared to this, and therefore designed to be addictive. There are lots of lovely flashing numbers and different bets all inviting you to come on in and play.

Come on, they shout, don't be an old fart like Robbie. Get stuck in and win!

But you should be really, really cagey about all these promises and invitations. Because spread betting can be addictive.

> Seriously, if you have already lost money playing casino sites, and you constantly lose money on the horses, and think you may already have a gambling problem, *steer well clear.*

It *is* very exciting watching the profits mount up! But you can lose a lot, and really quickly too. Don't just try spread betting because you tried everything else and lost. You'll lose at this too. And the problem here is, if you have any kind of gambling problem deep down inside you, spread betting will bring it out. And quickly. If after a couple of weeks you suddenly realise you made 50 trades, and are losing money – STOP!

Think carefully – have you become a gambler, and do you have a gambling problem? If you suspect you have, know deep down that you have, or possibly *think* that you might have, the wisest thing is to stop. Completely.

I'm not saying stop just because you started losing: it is possible to start with a few losses but then go into profit. I'm saying stop if you feel there is any kind of gambling problem developing. In the crash of 2008 a lot of people lost a lot of money spread betting, and a lot of those were gamblers.

If you do get into any sort of gambling problems with spread betting, or you feel out of control with it, contact Gamblers Anonymous (just Google it). Also take a look at www.gambleaware.co.uk.

Can you afford it?

The message is simple: if you can't afford to spread bet, then don't. If, for example, you fancy putting in a grand but can't afford to lose it – DON'T!!!!! [Robbie, easy on the exclamation marks, ink costs money. – Ed]

Only spread bet with money you really can afford to lose. Because, as I just mentioned, people in the past have lost *lots* spread betting, including their houses. Spread betting debts are enforceable by law. So think carefully before opening an account.

Okay, preaching over (but I do worry about people).

★   ★   ★

 Now, before London cab drivers can get a licence they need The Knowledge. Without The Knowledge they are likely to get lost and make a tit of themselves. Same with spread betting – if you don't have the knowledge you're likely to make a tit of yourself. So the following few sections cover the knowledge you will need to start spread betting.

2. The Knowledge: I

Spread Betting Compared to Normal Share Dealing

I'm assuming you have bought a share before, either on the phone or more likely online using one of the many execution-only brokers out there. There are many small differences of detail between trading in shares and spread betting, but here are the three main big differences:

1. There is no market

When you trade shares you deal through a stockbroker, who acts as an intermediary to pass your order through to the market (where the market is comprised of other buyers and sellers and market makers). When you spread bet, you deal directly with a spread betting firm – there is no market and the spread betting firm is acting as a principal not as an intermediary. This is important for three reasons:

1. Because the trade does not have to be passed through to a market, orders can be dealt very quickly.

2. You have to take the price made by the spread betting firm, though of course you can shop around between the firms.

3. Because the spread betting firm is acting as a principal you are at risk if the spread betting firm gets into trouble (the risk is very small, but it is still there).

2. Trading on margin

If you buy £5000 of shares and the share price then falls 20% you lose £1000. This is never pleasant, but it is unlikely to be terminal. But if you put up £5000 for a spread bet and the price falls 20% then you could lose £6600 – perhaps more.

The reason is that when you spread bet you are trading on margin, where you only need to put up a fraction of the value of the trade in actual cash. This gives you leverage – which can be great if the market goes your way, and nasty if it doesn't (similar to buying a house with a very big mortgage).

So, the risk associated with spread betting is far greater than when trading shares. And because of this, you have to learn different techniques when spread betting to control that risk. Techniques such as using stop orders. I'll be talking a lot about this later in the book.

3. Shorting

The third big difference with share trading is that with spread betting you can easily short shares – in other words make money when shares fall. As a trader if you don't short shares occasionally (i.e. you always just go long), this is like fighting Mike Tyson with one arm tied behind your back. (Well, naturally I could take on Mike with just one arm – with my patented kick-in-the-balls-and-run-like-hell technique – but I'm assuming that most people would need two arms.)

So, let's get stuck in. First up, what are 'prices' in the spread betting world...?

Spread Betting Prices

Every company listed on the market has a share price. (I know you knew that, but I'm taking this right from the beginning. Don't start heckling me yet.) And you will know that there is a BUY price and a SELL price. Let's take a quote of a share at random – say, Aggreko (AGK).

You can see the real-time price on any number of websites. The data here is from www.advfn.com and shows us, amongst other things, that you can SELL at 549 and you can BUY at 551. This is shown by the Bid and Offer columns.

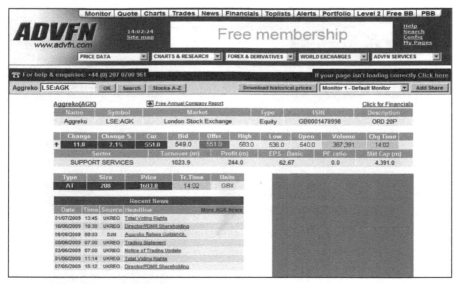

ADVFN screen showing Aggreko real-time price data

So if you want to buy Aggreko at this moment you would have to pay 551; if you wanted to sell it, it'd go for 549. Okay? Good. (Not okay? Then stop here till you've got it. If you can't get this bit, sell this book on eBay!)

The gap between the sell price and the buy price is called *the spread*. And that's why it's called *spread betting*! The spread betting firm makes money on the spread it charges you – the difference between the buy and sell price (the jargon for this is 'bid' and 'offer'). For example, if you buy Aggreko at 551, but then change your mind and decide to sell it immediately you will sell at 549; you lose 2 points in the trade – which is the profit made by the spread betting firm.

Let's now look at that in more depth.

Example

Aggreko's price is 549 to sell and 551 to buy. If you are looking at a real-time live share price, that is the *current market price*. So if you were to buy the share in the normal way it would cost you 551.

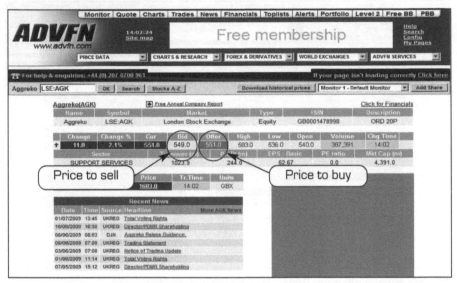

ADVFN price, buy and sell prices highlighted by arrows

Now let's see the price the spread betting firm is offering. In this instance, Tradefair:

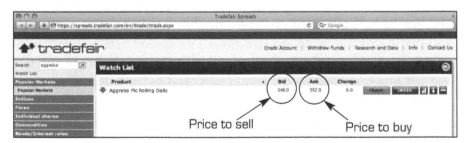

Tradefair screen, with rolling daily buy and sell prices

Product	Bid	Ask
Aggreko rolling daily	548	552

(Remember that *bid* and *ask* is just jargon for sell and buy.)

With the spread firm, you can see that the buy ('ask') and sell ('bid') prices are different from those offered in the share market – the gap between the spread betting prices is wider. If you want to buy, it will cost you 552p instead of 551p. And when you come to sell it again, you will be charged extra (wide) spread. This teeny little bit extra, going into and coming out of a stock, is a spread firm's constant source of profit.

So, the question is: why would you want to pay extra to 'buy' shares via spread betting, and then receive less when you sell, than with a comparable trade in the share market?

Good question!

The answer is because spread betting offers a number of attractions that outweigh those small extra wide spead costs, including:

• no commission

• no sales tax paid on purchases

• no capital gains tax

• the ability to short.

Placing a Spread Bet

Let's look now at placing a spread bet.

Buy or sell?

Take a look at Aggreko on Tradefair again. Press 'TRADE' next to, let's say, rolling daily.

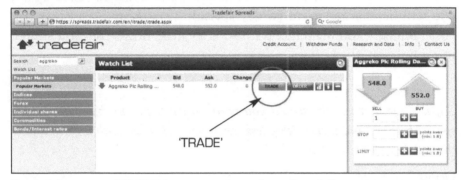

Tradefair screen, 'TRADE' button on Aggreko rolling daily

Now you can see sell (arrow down) at a price of 548, and buy (arrow up) at 552:

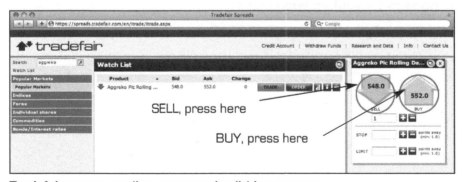

Tradefair screen, up/buy arrow and sell/down arrow

To buy it, you just press the up arrow; and to sell, you press the down one.

Trade size

But *before* that you also need to type in the amount you want to buy or sell in pounds per point (I will cover that a bit more in a mo). Once you've put in the amount and pressed buy or sell, a confirmation message will come up. Say you want a quid a point, tap in 1, then press the up arrow buy price and it's done. (You make a pound for every point Aggreko goes up.)

The confirmation message will say something like:

" *Bought £1 Aggreko at 552.* **"**

Then you're done. You've bought (or sold) and the next decision to make is when to sell your position and take a profit or loss. Which you could do right away if you wanted to, because your bet is now in your account's 'Open Positions' list.

However, let's pretend it's a week later and Aggreko moved up 20p.

Tradefair screen, open position, Aggreko now 20p higher

The Aggreko price is now 572-575. You are up 20 points at the new sell price (of 572). You sell and have made a £20 profit –

20 points x £1 = £20 profit

You can see this on the screen as your current profit or loss is always shown.

See the 'Trade' button again? Just press that, and then put in the exact opposite order to your original bet in order to close your position. (In this example, that would be *selling* at £1 a point.) The current profit or loss is then taken, and in this case your £20 is now banked!

Most spread-bet firms operate in a similar way, though some have specific 'Close' buttons. Always check you're certain of how to close out before opening a bet, to avoid needless panic or mistakes!

Let's take a look at an IG Index screen.

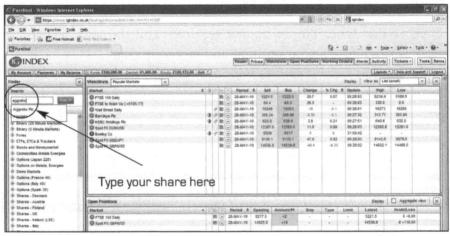

Standard initial IG screen

Type in the share you want – let's go for Aggreko again. I've done it here for the same share, but a year on.

This presents four different choices: daily rolling, or expiry over June, September or December. (Look at the 'Period' column.)

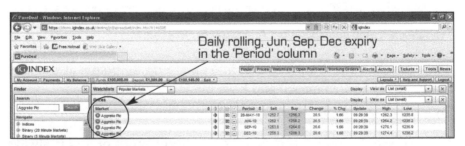

Four choices with the share

Click the one you want – let's go for June – and you can see that, like Tradefair, you type in your stake and press the sell or buy button together with your stop (if you want one). I'll explain the differences between a rolling and monthly expiry in a mo.

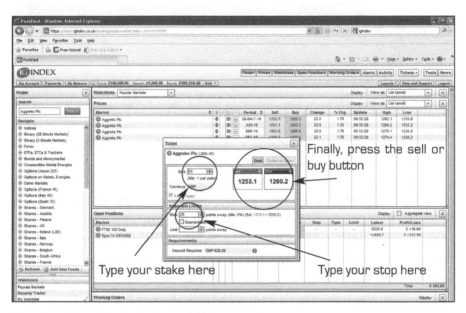

IG order ticket, Aggreko June expiry

All this expiry malarkey

The spread firm makes money whether your bet is a winner or a loser when it comes to closing it out. But, although you do get charged extra spread over what you would pay buying or selling shares in the normal way, remember: unlike normal trades there is no broker commission to pay, nor any stamp duty. So in the end there is not much in it, cost-wise.

However, **spread bets do tend to cost a bit more the longer you leave them open**, which is why they are usually considered to be for the shorter term; from a few days to a couple of months, maybe a bit longer.

In our earlier example we used a rolling daily bet on Aggreko: 'rolling' means the bet rolls over every day until you close it. The broker charges you a small amount overnight to keep it open (not much, something like 5p for a £1000 bet). Alternatively, most firms offer a 'quarterly expiry' – the spread is a bit wider but there is no daily charge.

So, in our Aggreko example:

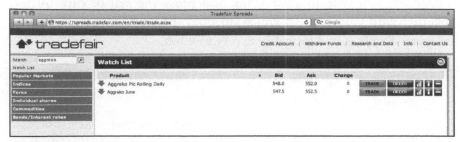

Tradefair screen showing Aggreko June expiry and rolling

Product	Bid	Ask
Aggreko rolling daily	548	552
Aggreko June	547.5	552.5

'June' here means a quarterly bet. It's called a 'quarterly bet' because there are four quarterly bets in a year that are introduced in sequence: March, June, September, December. Each of these bets expires in the third week of the month (e.g. June), when the new quarterly bet (e.g. September) will be introduced. So instead of being rolled over every day (as with the rolling bet), with quarterly there is no daily charge and it stays open until the expiry of the bet. However, as you can see, you pay a bit more spread than with the rolling bet.

If you are holding a June bet and want to keep the trade open beyond June, then you have to close the June bet and open a trade in the corresponding September bet. This is called 'rolling over' the bet, and can be done any number of times (e.g. the September bet could then be rolled over to the December bet). Each time a bet is rolled over the trader incurs the cost of the bid-offer spread – by closing one trade and opening another.

If your eyes are rolling and you're thinking, 'This is a bit complicated, why the different bets?' Don't worry, because I'm about to explain all this...

Different Types of Spread Bet

You might have noticed that I've mentioned terms like 'rolling bets' and 'quarterly bets'. (What do mean, you hadn't noticed – have you been paying attention or not?)

These are different type of spread bet. Luckily the difference between the types of spread bet can all be reduced to four little words: *It doesn't much matter!*

Really. It may matter to a 'professional' betting hundreds of thousands on a daily basis, but to you or me, with our small bets of, say, £100 to £500 or something like that, what will amount to a few quid here or there means *very* little. So **don't worry too much about whether you've got a rolling bet or a six monthly or a quarterly expiry**. You don't really need to lose sleep over whether you want a rolling bet or a quarterly expiry; there might be a few pence in it here or there, depending on how long you want to keep your bet open for, but that's it.

In the main, if you expect to keep the bet open for quite a while then you may as well go for the next quarter month, or even six months away (paying a bit more spread). If you intend to keep it open for a couple of weeks or so, go for rolling. Generally, rolling starts to get more expensive after about a fortnight.

It doesn't matter an awful lot. In fact, right now I am holding onto a rolling spread bet that has continued for nearly a YEAR! So what if it costs me a few pence every night? It's still going up!

 Recap

Let's hold on a sec here and recap:

- spread firms add a bit onto the spread, your cost, but there's no commission or stamp duty

- you can 'sell' without having bought first!

- to take your profit or loss just press the 'close' button

- rolling bets incur a small daily charge, quarterly bets have a bit more spread but no daily charge

- .. but don't worry too much about the type of bet unless you're a high roller.

Shorting

Let's assume you have a simple share dealing account with a stockbroker. Now, two questions –

Q1: If you own no shares in Aggreko and you think the shares are going to rise what can you do?

A: Ummm ... buy some shares. (Yes, that wasn't a trick question.) OK, now...

Q2: If you own no shares in Aggreko and you think the shares are going to fall what can you do?

A: Errr...

Exactly, errr. With a simple stockbroking account there's not much you can do. There might be a bear market, with nearly all share prices falling for a year or more and there's nothing much you can do about it.

But with super spread betting...

But with a spread betting account you can easily *sell* Aggreko *without* owning the shares, and so make money from it if you think it's going to go down.

Let's look at a quick example.

Example

Aggreko's spread bet price is 548-552, which means you can sell at 548 and buy at 552. You think the shares are going down so you sell at 548 for £5 a point to open a short position.

Two weeks latter the price has fallen to 522-526. To close the short position you must buy the bet back. The buy price is 526, so you buy the bet at that price for £5 a point – which closes the short position.

The result is you sold at 548 and then bought back at 526, making 22 points (548 - 526) which is a profit of £110 (22 points x £5).

What happens if I short a share and it goes bust?

Hey, it's good news! If you go short (bet on a share to go down) and it goes bust, you can burst into song: "We're in the money! We're in the money!" Alternatively, feel free to leap around the room.

But hang on a mo – you might just have to wait for a bit for the cash. The spread firm will want to ensure the share won't come back onto the market.

When administrators are appointed, that usually signifies the end. Spread firms will pay you out at 0! So, say in 2009 you were lucky enough to go short of Aero Inventory at 300 for a tenner a point, you'd be picking up a very nice profit of £3000.

On the whole these things take about two to three months to confirm – in the meantime your bet will just be frozen, but the payout should be worth the wait!

Staking

This is VERY important!

In the Aggreko example we had to decide how much to bet. First thing to remember: you are not buying a set number of shares, you trade in *pounds per point*. £1 per point, or a fiver a point, etc.

That means if you are betting on a share to go *up* at a fiver a point, every point (or one pence) it rises you make a fiver. But every pence it falls, you *lose* a fiver. The total profit or loss is then established when you decide to close the bet.

So say you buy a share at 500 for a fiver a point. It goes to 550 – you make £250, because it has risen 50 points (50 x £5).

Okay, easy enough to understand, but ... you MUST understand your *real* exposure to the share and whether or not you can afford to bet in the first place.

Equivalent number of shares

If you place a spread bet at 1p a point on a company, this is the equivalent of owning one share in that company: if the company's share price increases, say, 10p, then the share owner makes 10p and so does the spread bettor (10 points x 1p).

If you place a spread bet at 2p a point on a company, this is the equivalent of owning two shares in that company: if the company's share price increases, say, 10p, then the share owner (of two shares) makes 20p and so does the spread bettor (10 points x 2p). And so on...

The calculation of the equivalent number of shares is simply the number of pence bet per point (because 1p = 1 point).

So, if you place a spread bet at £1 a point on a company, this is the equivalent of owning 100 shares in that company (£1 = 100 x 1p).

And if you place a spread bet at £10 a point on a company, this is the equivalent of owning 1000 shares in that company (£10 = 1000 x 1p). If the company's share price increases, say, 5p, then the share owner makes £50 (5p x 1000 shares) and the spread bettor also makes £50 (5 points x £10).

All fine and dandy, but now we must look at exposure.

Exposure

If you buy 1000 shares in Company A whose share price is 10p, you will pay £100. And if you buy 1000 shares in Company B whose share price is £10, you will pay £10,000. The difference in your exposure is immediately obvious: in the first case you have £100 at risk, in the second case you have £10,000 at risk. If the share price of company A falls 5% your holding will fall £5 in value; while if the share price of company B falls 5% your holding will fall £500 in value. If you are worried that your exposure to company B may be too high, then you would not have bought so many shares in the first place.

All this is straightforward in the share market.

But exposure is not so obvious in spread betting because the full value of the share exposure is not paid up front. Instead one merely places a bet at so much per point. It's as easy to place a £10 per point bet on either Company A or Company B – but the risk exposure is very different!

This can be seen in the following table that compares the varying exposures resulting from a £10 a point bet on four companies with different share prices. The three columns are:

i – the share price of the company (for example, Company D has a share price of £20)

ii – a 10% move in the share price will result in the price moving this amount (expressed in pence)

iii – the profit or loss of a £10 per point bet on this company's share.

	Share price (p)	10% price move (p)	Effect on bet of £10/point (£)
	(i)	(ii)	(iii)
Company A	10	1	10
Company B	100	10	100
Company C	500	50	500
Company D	2000	200	2000

Sample spread bet exposures

If you buy the bet at £10/point on **Company A** and the share rises 10% you make £10, and if the share falls 10% you lose £10.

But if you buy the bet at £10/point on **Company D** and the share rises 10% you make £2000, and if the share falls 10% you lose £2000.

A loss of £10 or £2000 is a big difference – but they both result from the same size bet of £10!

Why?

Referring back to the previous section ('Equivalent number of shares'), when you open a bet at £10 a point, this is similar to holding 1000 shares in the company.

• 1000 shares of **Company A** (share price = 10p) is worth £100

• 1000 shares of **Company D** (share price = 2000p) is worth £20,000.

Looking at it this way, it may be easier to understand the effect of a 10% move in the share prices, and thereby how different exposures can result from the same size bet.

 You MUST work out your exposure *every* time.

Using the earlier Aggreko example, if you bet £10/point when the Aggreko price is 552, then your exposure will be £5520 (£10 x 552).

I get tons of emails saying something like,

" *Oh, I always stick on a tenner a point.* **"**

But £10 on a 20p share = £200 exposure. On a 1000p share it's £10,000! Beware!

 Tip: You ought to add up the total exposure in your spread bet portfolio. Would you have taken that much exposure in standard trading?

You MUST understand this staking!

Gottit? If not, stop here until you have.

And before you put a bet on ask yourself: can I afford this stake? What if it goes bust (or, if shorting, goes through the roof)? If the worst comes to the worst can I afford to pay the spread firm if I lose?

Say you had bought £10 a point at 1000p a share and the share goes bust – you lose £10,000.

Phew! That's a lot to digest...

If you struggle with the above the bottom line to remember is:

£5 a point = the same as buying 500 shares

£10 a point = the same as 1,000 shares

£20 a point = the same as 2,000 shares.

If you don't quite get all the above yet, keep going through it until you do, especially staking!

Closing Bets

When you 'sell' a spread bet at, say, 70, you may be doing one of two things:

1. selling to close a bet that you have previously bought. For example, you may have previously bought at 50, and now want to sell at 70 and take the 20 profit. Or,

2. you may be opening a new short position at 70.

It goes without saying that it's important to know which of the above you intend!

A way of removing any ambiguity is to always refer to trades that close a position as 'closing trades' or 'closing bets'.

On most spread betting websites, where it displays your open positions, there will usually be a button by the side of each open position labelled 'close'. For example, if you had a long bet on Aggreko, on the web page you'd click 'close' by the side of the Aggreko position details, then a page current price would appear and you would click 'sell' to confirm the trade. This makes it easier for you to ensure you are closing the bet and not opening up a new one!

You don't have to close the whole bet

One thing that's vital to know is that you don't have to close your whole trade.

Let's say Aggreko was up 100 points, and you were in profit £1000 with a tenner per point stake. You think there might be further to go but you're not sure. You could, say, close half the position. To do this, you would put "5" in the close box instead of "10" – you then take £500 profit and keep a fiver a point of the bet running.

But it may be that you don't want to close a bet for a while; you may want to keep it open for some time. In which case, what do you do when the bet approaches expiry? You need to rollover (as the little one said)…

Rollovers

If you want to keep a spread bet open for a number of months, chances are you will have to rollover the bet. For example, if you buy a June bet in April, and want to hold the bet open to August, as the June gets close to expiry you will have to sell it and buy a later bet (e.g. the September bet). This is called *rolling over*.

You have till 4pm on the day of expiry (the third Tuesday in March, June, September, or December) to ask the spread-bet firm to roll your bet over to the next quarter or else your bet will expire.

> Note: Obviously, you don't have to rollover. In fact, it's not such a bad thing to let bets expire on expiry day as sometimes it's nice to clear out an account and take the profits and losses.

To rollover you need to call the spread-bet firm. However, it is best to rollover in the middle of the day rather than at the beginning, because you want the new spread to be as tight as possible. After all, a rollover means you are selling the stock and re-buying it, so the bid-offer spread counts. For example, if you have a share that is 450-456, but you know the spread has a tendency to narrow as the trading day progresses, then wait for it to narrow (perhaps to 455-456) before you call to roll it over.

The firms usually give you a discount on the old and new bet to encourage you to roll, so you do get a cheaper price than if you just sold and then bought it back.

Margin

With a normal sharedealing account with a stockbroker you can only buy shares up to the value of cash you've got in your account. But with spread betting you can bet more than the funds available in your account. This is because when you open a spread bet you don't have to put up the full value of the trade, you just put up a fraction of it. The fraction you put up is called *margin* – although it could equally be called DANGER.

Small margin, big exposure

Let's look at our favourite Aggreko again.

If you buy a spread bet on Aggreko at 552 for £10 per point, then your exposure will be £5520 (£10 x 552). Now, in the ordinary share market, to get an exposure of £5520 you would have to put up... £5520! But in the spread bet here you would only have to put up around £828 (roughly 15% of the trade value of £5520).

You might be thinking: "well, that's very nice, but what about the remaining £4692 (5520 – 828), who's covering that?" The answer is: your spread betting firm. They are in effect providing you with £4692 of credit.

With most top shares, spread firms only expect the funds in your account to cover some of the bet. With a liquid stock like Aggreko, chances are you will only be charged about 15% of the total value, therefore you only need to put about £1500 in your account to enable a £10,000 exposure.

It's slightly different with smaller cap stocks; since smaller companies are more illiquid, the margin rate will be higher. So for a small cap you could easily be charged 50% instead, meaning you'd have to put up £5000 to get exposure of £10,000.

Maintaining the margin

Let's say you buy a bet at 500 for £20 a point. Your total exposure will therefore be £10,000 (500 x £20). And to fund this trade you have to put up £1500 (15% of £10,000). Now, let's look at two cases:

- If the market **rises** 50 points, you make £1000 on the trade (50 x £20), and this £1000 is credited to your account with the spread betting firm. But,

- if the market **falls** 50 points, you lose £1000. This £1000 is deducted from your margin account, leaving just £500 (£1500 - £1000). But your spread betting firm requires you to have £1500 in your account to cover this trade, so they will ask you to deposit another £1000 in your account to make it back it up to £1500. This is called a *margin call* – something that no trader wants to get.

The danger of margin

While trading on margin is a great attraction of spread betting, **treat the margin with care. Otherwise you could get into trouble.**

Let's say, for example, you go over the top and have £50,000 of exposure in your spread-bet account, whilst only putting up £10,000. The market suddenly tanks badly whilst you are away for the day. Your shares bomb, and you don't have enough in your account to cover your losses. The spread firm leaves you messages asking for money – they want £15,000 immediately. You look in your bank account and gulp – you only have £5000 in there and you can't pay them.

This is never a position you want to be in. *Don't ever overexpose yourself.* If you can't afford all the positions at 100% loss in your account, or you could not afford to stump up all the cash if it was suddenly demanded of you, you MUST reduce the size of your positions immediately.

Remember, the spread firms will expect you to wire the money immediately, not tomorrow. If you can't afford to pay them, they can – and just might – start closing out all of your positions immediately.

So use the leverage with care, and don't use all of it unless you have lots of money sitting about to cover possible losses.

More on margin and leverage

I was invited to dinner by an excellent trader, someone who had been successful with spread betting. I asked him why he thought so many people came a cropper with spread betting – and indeed why some people who were reasonably successful trading normal accounts couldn't do the same with spread betting. He said –

" *That's an easy one, they use the leverage.* **"**

Just one sentence, but he summed it up well.

What he means is that when people build up their spread betting accounts and start to make a profit, they have access to bigger and bigger bets.

When things can get nasty...

Let's say someone kicked off by sticking £5000 in a spread betting account – this could give him exposure to £50,000 worth of shares.

So, he uses all the leverage. His £5000 covers trades of value £50,000. And he feels okay about this because he has, say, £15,000 in his bank account that he can afford to lose. He has a good run and, wow, he can now buy around £80,000 of shares and the profits are rolling in! Then there is a sudden downturn – a lot of his shares tumble badly, he panics and buys some more shares with the leverage in order to average down, but they go down too.

Now, suddenly, he is in trouble.

He realises he owes the spread firm £30,000 – that's £15,000 more than he can put his hands on.

The phone rings.

He knows it's the spread firm. He panics again and ignores the call. Shares tumble further; the spread firm starts closing out his trades, as it is entitled to do, because he owes a lot of money. Now he's really getting in trouble. He can't buy any more shares to average down, or to try to get himself out of the mess. The spread firm emails him a few times saying *all* his positions will be closed unless he adds some money to his account.

He goes for it and uses his bank card to wire over the £15,000 that he has in his account. Now he can trade a little more. And he does, with more disastrous consequences, not helped by his state of mind. He now owes £40,000.

> **Note:** Spread-bet losses are enforceable by law.

The phone keeps ringing.

He knows he can't pay. The spread firm closes down the rest of his trades and now he has to work out how to pay the bill without his wife finding out he lost.

So, you see this is where too much leverage can get you.

The case of Nick Levene, who famously lost £50 million-plus spread betting, shows how big debts can mount up – quickly.

Spread firms have actually put some structures in place to try and stop this happening, and will call and email you very fast if you go over your limit. Even so, the above scenario could still happen.

Here are my thoughts on leverage.

You have £15,000 you can afford to lose and you want to spread bet. Put £5000 into the spread account. This could give you access to £50,000 of shares. But only use a little of that leverage. In this situation, ensure you only give yourself access to £20,000 of shares. Once you have too much exposure, close out some positions or bank profits.

The s**t hitting the fan

In 2008, a lot of trouble happened for spread bettors. Because liquidity in the markets was vanishing, overnight many spread firms cut the amount of margin allowed. So, for instance, instead of allowing your 15% margin on Aggreko, now they wanted 40% – and suddenly you either had to pay up or close the position!

It was worse for small caps. Some firms that had been allowing 30% margin on small caps now called clients and said that they were moving margins to 90%! In other words, clients now had to stump up pretty much all the cash for that position immediately or it would be closed.

www.petedredge.co.uk

I got many emails from stunned spread bettors saying: "How could they do this to me just like that?"

Well, the answer is: because they can!

They don't have to give you margin and they can change their minds at *any time*. The spread firms were changing margins because they were worried that clients were going to end up owing them money, and although spread-bet losses are enforceable by law, they didn't want clients leaving them holding the baby.

They were actually right.

Many spread punters have gone under, in some cases owing huge sums they simply cannot pay back. It's the usual story. If you owe someone £10,000 it's your problem. If you owe someone £1 million it's their problem!

www.petedredge.co.uk

This is from the *Daily Telegraph*:

> 66 *The Conservative Party treasurer has been forced to inject £70m of his own personal wealth into City Index after traders defaulted on tens of millions of pounds of trades. Accounts filed at Companies House late last week reveal that clients of the spread betting business were unable to cover £43m of losses after share prices collapsed. Just six clients accounted for the majority of the loss, with one client losing £29m betting on a single Spanish property company. Notes to the accounts reveal that another City Index client has lost a further £12m speculating on the markets, since the year end. To-date £4m of that debt has been recovered.* 99

Other spread firms reported clients unable to pay, too, with IG Index recording around £16 million of client losses to be recouped.

Do NOT allow this to ever happen to you. Limit your exposure by not leveraging your account to the full amount possible.

The moral of the story is: *don't take excessive advantage of the margin;* the margin will soon take advantage of you.

And Finally, the Good Bit – Taking Profits

Take the moolah

It's exactly how to be a winner.

The worst thing to do is let a winning cash balance just build up, because it will tempt you into bigger and bigger bets – the downfall of so many spread bettors, as I've already discussed. So, if you do find yourself in the fortunate position of some nice wins, and therefore have a good positive cash balance in your spread-bet account, consider banking some of that cash. Stick it in a high-interest account or even buy premium bonds! Then you have really and truly banked some profits.

If you continue to leave a big cash balance in your spread betting account, you will be tempted to use some of it – with the consequence that you will at some point overstake or overtrade.

So just think,

'*I'm a banker.*'

Obviously don't say this out loud too often.

Withdrawing money

Remember: you can only withdraw available cash inside your account. Cash in there that is supporting your positions has to be left in. If you want to withdraw the lot, of course, you need to close all your positions. The spread firms will usually send you the money right away by bank transfer.

3. The Knowledge: II

The previous Knowledge section dealt with some specific technical details of spread betting. This second Knowledge section now broadens things out a bit to look at how best to approach spread betting.

Firstly, you might be thinking that if spread betting is such a great idea, why do anything else...

Why Shouldn't I Just Spread Bet and Nothing Else?

A bloke came to one of my seminars and asked this question in pretty much the same words. He then admitted that the answer he was looking for was a confirmation that, yes, all traders *should* just go ahead and exclusively spread bet.

But that's not an answer I could give.

In fact, it actually didn't matter what I said to him – I could see he was only going to spread bet and that was it. However, here's what I said anyway (because I am a kind soul):

“ *After years of getting emails and listening to people talking about their spread betting, I've found that the people that lose the most are those who just spread bet and nothing else.* **”**

My opinion is that you should use spread betting *only* as an addition to a sensible investment strategy. Because, although it's similar cost-wise to just buying shares normally, it is more addictive; and because you can see your losses and wins go up and down second by second, it is more tempting to overtrade.

There are also the ready pitfalls of using too much of the leverage and having too much exposure. So really, truly, don't do it just on its own.

Tax

At the time of writing, spread betting is currently tax-free. I suppose things could change in the future, but given more people lose than win it is very unlikely to ever be taxed.

You don't have to declare your profits, even if you win a lot. However, the only possible way they could try to tax you is if they can prove spread betting is your only and sole source of income.

As I have said, I hope with all readers here that this will not be the case. So there is the tiny chance of a possibility of a grey area here if you do just spread bet and nothing else. Another reason why I don't, by the way, think spread betting on its own is a good idea!

Someone helpfully relaid the following on my online bulletin board:

> ❝ HMRC is very reluctant to classify anyone as a professional gambler [but] it is its decision alone – not yours. Keep this link safe or print it off:
>
> www.hmrc.gov.uk/manuals/bimmanual/bim22017.htm
>
> The reason HMRC is reluctant to classify anyone as professional is that a professional gambler can claim relief against losses from gambling. ❞

So there you are. If you feel worried about any tax implication, ask, as they say, a suitably qualified person (this is NOT me!). Bottom line is it's very unlikely you will have to pay any tax on profits.

Real Money or Pretend Money?

This is a hard one to answer: Should you start to spread bet for real or just use pretend money in a demo account?

You might find my answer surprising: I think, real money.

But, only on the basis that you can genuinely afford to lose the money. Here is an interesting mail I got from a reader which shows how trading with fake money isn't always such a good idea:

&& In an attempt to hedge some of my losses, I have been learning about spread betting via a demo site and am ashamed to say that I have whittled down a £10k account to £125 within a few months, with rash bets and poorly judged punts! Knowing that it wasn't real money promoted this cavalier approach, but now I wish to do it properly. &&

Interesting. Trading fake money can make you more gung-ho. Trouble is, this reader might carry on with the same approach once he's using real money, so disaster lurks.

Or, you could argue, the disaster with the demo account will make him more careful with real money. A tricky one. Obviously if you don't have the funds yet to open a spread betting account, you are going to have to use a demo platform, or alternatively paper trade.

The most common criticism of paper trading is that while paper trading allows one to learn some basic technical skills it doesn't deal with the big issues of controlling emotions and being disciplined. When you have real money on the line, it can change how you behave – and *that's* what beginner traders need to control. Paper trading doesn't help there.

One idea could be to try and start with really small stakes – £1 a point is usually allowed by most firms. One firm called Finspreads offers readers the chance to bet at just 10p a point for a while – see the offer at the end of the book. At least it's real money but not big enough for you to lose much. It seems to me, judging from feedback I have received, that in the end it's better to go with real money.

How much money do you need to get started?

Ah, that's a tricky one. Generally, not that much if you want to try spread betting. Indeed, it's better if you start with just small stakes. The key, whatever the amount, is that it's money you can afford (and are prepared) to lose.

£1000 would get you access to over £5000-worth of exposure. That might be a good start. BUT only if you actually have a further £5000 in cash. Please don't get yourself £5000 exposure with only £1000 of readies – you are asking for trouble if you cannot cover your losses.

Ultimately it's not something I would really care to advise you on, as it depends on what your assets and cash flow are and how much you can afford to lose.

I would, however, suggest that whatever money you put in, you mentally say goodbye to it and pretend you no longer have it.

Spread Betting Systems and Bulletin Boards

I get many approaches from companies who want to advertise their amazing get-rich-quick spread betting systems on my website, and I turn them all down. They make amazing claims along the lines of "guaranteed profits", "turn £2000 into £75,000 with two minutes work a day", etc.

Remember: all these claims sound too good to be true because, er, they are!

One bloke who came to a seminar of mine had paid £2000 for a system which lost him £23,000! He was gutted (who wouldn't be?). It was a specialist spread betting system that had boasted of great profits. He won to start off with, then gradually his money went down the drain. Yet, despite the money disappearing, he still believed in the system.

My top tip for readers who want to avoid becoming poor *very* quickly: don't believe in systems.

The moment you enter the world of spread betting your inbox will get deluged with offers from people wanting to sell you systems or tips. And you'll see lots of ads around, shouting about "How I made a million: let me show you how I did it". Or any other line they think will hook you in: "Money Trend Systems" or "SuccessTrades" or whatever.

All are hogwash.

Being human, these kinds of ads and emails are very seductive. You may think, "Ooh goody, the system will do the work for me." But you're just being lazy. I'm pretty lazy too, so I quite understand, but this kind of laziness will empty your bank account fast.

A lot of these system operators are surprised that I don't want to advertise them. "You really don't want the money?" Well, no! Because I don't believe in them so I don't want to be a hypocrite. Hence you won't find any ads for spread betting systems on my site. If you do, it probably means I just lost a lot of money spread betting, and am trying to save the house!

I suggest – at least until you know what you're doing – that you completely ignore the very idea of a system and concentrate on working out how to spread bet. Make trades for yourself. Take time to do that. Then gradually devise your *own* system (i.e. your own systematic approach). This will cost you nothing and will be far more rewarding.

Bulletin boards

There are many online bulletin boards (are they called forums nowadays?) devoted to trading financial markets. It can be helpful to read some of them regarding the share you are looking to trade, but unfortunately many of them appear to be like a brawl in a pub, with people who don't even know each other wading in to punch as many people as possible with their strong-minded opinions.

However, some are dedicated to spread betting and you may pick up some useful hints. The one thing you ought to be aware of, especially if you are dealing in the smaller companies, is that there are gangs (perhaps even paid-for people) who pump up or slag off companies to try to influence your trading. Take everything you read with a massive pinch of salt. And don't believe anything you read until you verify it for yourself.

At my seminars I have heard any number of tales of woe from people who've bought bets on companies because someone on a bulletin board said it would be a "multibagger" or "the deal is just around the corner".

Some have lost an awful lot of money trusting anonymous strangers on bulletin boards and some have even had companies that went bust on them. So use bulletin boards if you want to – but please regard everything with a sceptical eye.

Charting

I used to pooh-pooh the idea of using charting mumbo jumbo to help to make money spread betting. However, I have met some people (well, two) who do use it to some effect. Since one is just a genius and the other uses it in conjunction with fundamentals and other ideas, I am still not completely sold. I've happily made a lot of money spread betting without using charts.

I have to say I am not an expert on charting (also called technical analysis). I do have some knowledge of it, but this book is about starting spread betting and if you are relatively new then it may be simpler to concentrate on fundamentals, at least to begin with.

However, what TA can do is instil some discipline, which can only be a good thing.

But how does technical analysis work and what's it all about?

It's the study of charts, or the price history of a share or index. The idea is that history, and particular ways of filtering or analysing that history, can forecast the future price direction. Personally, I don't believe you should use it 100% and ignore all the other factors in the market, but as an extra tool in your armoury it's worth looking at. Whether it is worth spending money on expensive TA systems and tools I don't know, but it's rare that I get a mail from anyone saying they just used TA on its own and made money over time, and I don't think I've ever had a mail from someone saying they purchased a system that had made them a fortune.

If you decide studying charts is for you, you'll need to buy some books and learn about it, and then decide whether to buy any extra equipment to help you analyse charts. One way I use TA is through my use of ADVFN Top Lists, as I think shares breaking up or down through a range over a year or half-year are worth noting – but I get this for £60 a year! (Mail me if you want this for less as ADVFN will lob you a discount via me.)

To start with it's worth looking at resistance and support levels on charts. Quite simply, these are price levels where a share tends to stop rising and where it tends to stop falling. At this point it is all about herd mentality and I think there is merit in looking at these, as explained elsewhere in the book.

Then there are chart patterns – shapes which some say predict what happens next. A 'head and shoulders' is the most commonly sought and is supposed to signal a move down. It's where a share has risen a lot, comes down, goes back up again and then starts another run down. I discuss a lot of these chart patterns in *The Naked Trader* and there is some merit in looking at them.

TA fans also use moving averages. This has more of a mathematical basis, with one favourite being the 200-day average. A moving average is worked out by adding the prices over a number of days and then dividing that figure by the number of days. If a price rises above the moving average it's considered bullish and if it goes below then it's bearish. Luckily software systems can do all the number crunching for you.

The biggest problem for TA fans is that there are just *so* many indicators. Which should you use? You can't follow all of them. The bulletin boards are full of confused traders trying this, that or the other indicator. I think you can end up getting caught up in it all and I see people spending so much time analysing indications they hardly ever get a trade on!

For example, I got an email from someone who tried to use TA on its own for eight years but never made any real money. He wrote:

66 I buy when the price crosses the moving averages, the heiken ashi candle changes colour, sometimes I wait for the parabolic SAR to reverse, and now I wait for the ADX to be over 20, and the DMI lines to cross... 99

I don't know what he's talking about either! All I know is he didn't make any money! So my thoughts are: charts are worth looking at but don't use them on their own.

Dealing With Your Spread Betting Firm

Problems with getting through

It doesn't happen that often but sometimes I get emails from people who had trouble getting a trade on or closing it out – a website freezes or the trade is rejected. This is usually because it is near the end of the day (say 4.15pm to 4.30pm), and so many people are trying to trade that sometimes computers can't keep up. So if you're thinking of closing, it's worth thinking about doing it before everyone else does.

Another problem occurs in a fast-moving market. A news story or event has happened and a price is moving up or down very fast (this can often happen with indices). You are pressing the button for a price, but at the moment you press it, the price has already moved again – and so the trade is rejected. In these situations it is often worth using a very old-fashioned method of interaction known as a fixed-line telecommunications device (AKA a telephone). Call the dealing desk, which should give you a quote there and then. You can accept and they will do the trade for you. So if in doubt, CALL!

Complaints against a firm

So, you made a bet and you feel you got stopped out wrongly. Or they reckon you made a bet and you think you didn't. Whatever your complaint is, the first thing is to phone the firm and put your case. The spread firms will always correct something if they got it wrong. They don't wish to annoy their customers, after all.

However, if they refuse to put right what you think is wrong, your next step is an email or letter to the boss of the firm. Put your case firmly and don't be rude. You'd be wise to avoid addressing your complaint to "You ****** bunch of ******", etc, etc. (Just a tip, that one.)

If you still get no joy, you can contact the FSA. It runs an arbitration scheme and your complaint will be independently assessed. It shouldn't ever get to that. On the rare occasion a spread firm has made a mistake on my account, it has always been resolved fairly.

It is worth checking each trade as it appears in your account, after you put it on, to ensure it is right. But I must say after years of emails from people complaining about things like their stops getting hit and moaning it was the spread firm's fault, I rarely find a case where the firm was *really* at fault. After all, the stops are generally hit by the computers, not someone sitting there doing it manually.

Tips and Advice

The daily trading timetable

What time of day is best to spread bet?

Well, the UK market tends to be busy for the first couple of hours and then slows down. It then speeds up again after 1.30pm when the US futures start to turn over and sometimes US economic stats are published. It gets even busier once the Dow opens at 2.30pm, goes a bit quiet between 3pm and 4pm, and then there is usually a mad dash to the close. Betting right at the opening bell of 8am is dangerous as spreads can be wide early doors.

What day of the week is better?

There isn't one really. However, day traders refer to Fridays as "Traders' graveyard day". I think possibly with the weekend break coming up a lot of trades get closed early Friday afternoon so shares tend to go down towards the close of play on Fridays.

Holding times

Although spread betting is often thought of as being for shorter-term trading it is also useful for longer-term trades, and if a share keeps on going up I will be happy to carry on holding it as a spread bet. Indeed, one of my bigger spread bet wins was a share I held for two years!

Day trading

I was intending to sum up day trading in one word: DON'T!

(Oh, wouldn't that have been so terribly witty, darling?)

But that's unfair. True, more than 90% lose at this (as David Brent would say, "fact") however, some – not many – but some *do* succeed, so I decided I ought to mention it. Indeed my friend Richard is a brilliant day trader but he is one of the few who have the necessary discipline and concentration to be successful.

Day trading generally means closing out positions by the end of each day, leaving no positions open overnight. The idea is to exploit short-term, intraday moves. Day traders don't care much about any share's prospects longer than what it might do today. Tomorrow doesn't matter.

It has a kind of appeal and I can certainly see the attraction. Indeed, some people hold long-term portfolios but day trade as well, often using spread betting for the short-term trades. But it isn't for me. I just don't have the concentration needed – and nor do I want to be tied to a desk all day (a bed is, perhaps, another matter).

If you are going to go in for this form of trading, I would just do it and nothing else; you really need to concentrate on this full time. I cannot imagine how you could have a job and day trade. And if you are going to day trade, you need a particular kind of strategy ... and it's pointless asking me, as I have no interest in it and think it's the way to the poor house!

Your time

Time is money, as they say.

When thinking about spread betting you need to look at how much time you have to execute and check your trades during working hours (I'm assuming here that you have a job). I've got a friend who's a dentist and he trades shares between patients. He's a great dentist –

though I make sure I don't get treated on a bad market day when his shares are going down.

The question is: *if you don't have very much time during the day, should you be spread betting?*

I have heard of people trying to spread bet who don't even have access to share prices during the day because their firewall at work prevents them from accessing the relevant sites, or their bosses don't allow any internet access at all. So what they do is place orders with spread-bet companies in the evening to be activated the next day. Don't even consider this.

If you really can't get access during the day you could look at spread betting US markets instead, as they are open in the evening.

But to spread bet, in my opinion, you need access to market prices for at least small periods of time *regularly* throughout the day. Spread bets do need to be looked at, nurtured and cared for! If time is very limited, then don't take on too many bets.

Which brings me to...

Number of bets

Spread bet traders often come unstuck when they have too many positions open. My view is that ten is more than enough.

I've seen some traders who have 60 positions open!

This is madness – especially if things become volatile. It's a bit like living in a house that's a total mess and you can't find anything – eventually it drives you crazy. With that many open, a trader will just get overwhelmed – psychologically as well as financially.

However, around ten positions is nice and neat and such a number can be easily looked after.

One possibility, if you are happy to have short as well as long positions, is to have longs with one company and shorts with another. Some traders find that having shorts and longs mixed into one account is a bit mind-blowing, although personally it doesn't bother me.

So, my view is stick to around ten positions – and certainly 15 max.

Plan each and every trade

If you have a pint or two for lunch and come back to your spread betting account and stick a trade on for the sake of it, you'll almost probably end up losing your dosh. You must resist rushes of blood to the head. You must have a good reason for making every single trade.

Before placing every trade you must know:

• why are you buying or shorting this share or index?

• how much are you prepared to lose on it?

• what is your stop loss?

• what is your target price?

If you haven't already thoroughly worked these out, put down the mouse, step away from the computer (and maybe go back to the pub).

Watch for ex-dividend days!

One thing to remember is ex-dividend dates. That's because your share will go down at the market opening by whatever the dividend is. So if it's a 10p dividend, the chances are the share will open down 10p.

This is important to know – some spread firms have the dividend in the price when you buy it and some don't. Some pay you the dividend. Be careful and make sure you don't sell the share or it doesn't hit a stop just because it has gone ex-dividend. Shares typically rise pretty quickly after the ex-date, often back to where they were.

How do you know the ex-dividend date?

They are always in the company's last statement, and also most websites that carry market data mark the shares with 'XD' by it. It's just worth making a note of when the XD is on any trade to be sure you remember. It's amazing the number of people who sell on an ex-dividend date. I get countless emails from people who go "D'oh! I took a loss/profit on a spread bet just when I shouldn't, because it went ex-dividend!"

So, check your dates. Shares nearly always go ex-dividend on a Wednesday, so that's the key day to watch.

Also, don't try to be clever. Everyday an email arrives in my inbox which says something like –

> " Aha! I have a foolproof plan to make money. If a share price goes down on ex-dividend day then all I have to do is short it the day before it goes ex-dividend and make money every time. "

Come on! You didn't really think you'd discovered a foolproof way to make money out of Mr Market did you?

The spread-bet firms all make sure you can't do this. As mentioned above, the dividend was already in the price when you shorted or else if you go short you have to pay out the dividend! Don't even think about it, clever clogs.

4. The Great Stop Order

Stop Losses

You may have heard about these – but what are they? Stop losses are orders that are activated when you say "enough is enough", and take your loss on the chin before it gets any bigger.

This is such an important topic – I refer to stop orders constantly throughout this book – that I thought it deserves its own chapter.

Before diving into the detail of stop orders, let's first look at a simple share investment made by an investor, who we will call Bob.

Bob and his shares that were going to the moon

The following chart shows the share price for a company – for the moment it's not important to know the name of the company. Bob has been following this company and notes that while the shares had been stuck in a horizontal range for much of 2003-2005, the price then broke out of the range from around mid-2006 and started heading up. Bob liked this type of situation and decided to pile in if the shares broke through the 600 level.

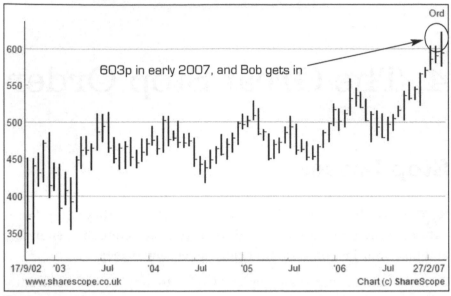

On the up and up

As can be seen, the price duly rose through 600 and Bob ended up buying some shares at 603p at the beginning of 2007. In the following couple of months the price moved around a bit but basically looked to be continuing the trend higher. Bob felt pretty smart. *Surely – next stop 700, and then on to the moon.*

And then...

Okay, not ideal. Things start going down. *Surely just a temporary correction, though...*

A 'temporary correction'

"Typical, typical, typical," thought Bob, "I always seem to buy at the high". However, he wasn't overly concerned as he knew that prices never went up in a straight line. The chart showed clearly that the uptrend was still in place and this still was just a temporary correction.

And then...

Oh bugger

"Hmmm," thought Bob, "that's not so good. In fact, bugger!"

However, Bob was damned if he was going to sell now and take a 30% loss. He reasoned that the shares were sitting solidly on a support level of around 420 – indeed they had most recently shown signs of bouncing off from this level. If he sold now, he just knew the shares would rocket up and he'd end up feeling stupid and cheesed off. No, reasoned Bob, these shares were still a good investment; it was just a case of holding one's nerve and sitting tight.

And then...

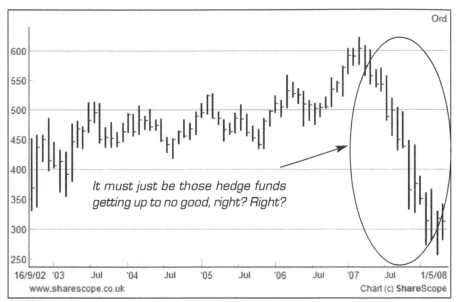

Double bugger

"Double bugger!" Bob was really annoyed now. "What the heck is going on here? This is ridiculous! There's no way these shares are worth just 300p now when they were worth over 600p just a few months ago." Bob had read something about hedge funds shorting the shares which had driven the price down, and while he didn't understand the exact details of that he thought it was exactly the sort of irresponsible thing that hedge funds *would* do.

At least the shares seemed to have consolidated at the 300 level. And, anyway, there is absolutely *no way* that he was going to sell at a 50% loss when the shares were obviously worth 600 and had been just temporarily depressed by the actions of a bunch of shysters.

And then...

Well, that could have gone better.
I hear stamp collecting can be fun.

Game over

"Triple bugger!"

Two years after buying the shares★, the price was 24p. A fall of 96% from 603p. Bob still owned his shares, but was "fed up with this stupid share stuff".

Money or balls

The above is a good case study in how not to invest; there are many things that Bob did wrong.

One thing we can observe is how good Bob was at rationalising his bad decisions. All investors – especially bad ones – can be extremely creative in coming up with excuses for why they are not wrong.

Quick question: is the purpose of investing,

1. to make money, or

2. to prove you have bigger balls than Gordon Ramsay?

If you answered (2), then put this book down right now!

★ The shares we have been looking at are those of the marvellous Royal Bank of Scotland.

You must realise that (1) and (2) are rarely compatible when it comes to investing. Humility is the order of the day: accept your mistakes and quickly move on.

How stop losses work

So, what should Bob have done instead?

The answer: use a stop loss.

Let's look again at the chart at the time that Bob bought his shares.

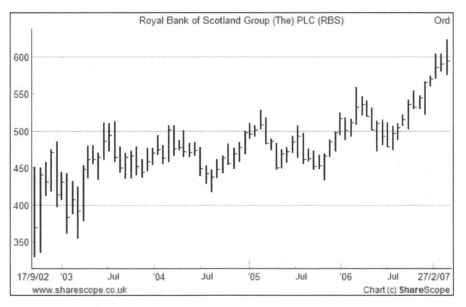

The folly of Bob

After Bob had bought his shares, he should have placed another order with his broker that said something like: "if the price falls to 500 then sell all my shares". That is a stop order!

Now, the question of what exact level to set as the trigger point to sell the shares is a big topic (one that I look at later in this book). There are several levels that could be considered, for example:

- 550 – this was roughly the high set at the beginning of 2006
- 520 – this was the top level of the horizontal trading range from 2003-2005

- 500 – a round number that might act as support for the shares

- 490 – a few points below the round number 500

- 440 – roughly the lower level of the horizontal trading range from 2003-2005.

And then there are any number of other possible levels; levels determined with reference to moving averages, trend lines, Bollinger Bands, etc.

A whole book could be written on where to set the trigger level for stop orders. The purpose of the trigger level is to set it at a level where you say, "OK, this doesn't seem to be working I'd better get out just in case".

But the crucial point at the moment is that finessing the trigger level is of second-degree importance – the most vital thing is to set a stop order in the first place!

 A bad stop order (and it is difficult to know how to define a bad stop order exactly) is better than no stop order at all.

Mental stops don't work

So, a stop order is a precise order that you give to your broker.

There are some traders who think that they don't need to place such an order; they believe they can monitor the performance of the shares themselves, and if the shares go down they will sell them. But this requires a level of discipline that is beyond most people. We saw in the example of poor Bob how easy it is to rationalise our mistakes in the heat of the moment. There is always an explanation or excuse for just about every situation. Avoid this trap – please!

One of the useful features of a stop order is that it is an order that can be placed when we are thinking rationally; it can even be placed when the markets are closed. So, we can and should determine ahead of time what is the critical level below which, should things fall, we will accept it is best to get out with our shirts still on our backs. (Steady...)

Stop losses to limit losses

In the example above, if Bob had invested £1000 in the shares at 603p, his holding would have been worth £40 two years later. A loss of £960.

Bad news.

Whereas, if he had placed a stop order with a trigger at 500p, his broker would have sold his shares when the price fell to 500. This would have incurred a loss of 17% (or £170). Nasty – but much better than losing 96%.

That's the key thing – avoid the big losses. And that's where stop losses are useful.

 Academic studies [hey, wake up at the back, this is important stuff!] show that the important thing in investing is not to beat the index by a few points when prices are rising, but rather to avoid the big losses when markets fall.

Stop losses and spread betting

If stop losses are important for ordinary share investing (and I hope I've convinced you of that!), then they are a hundredfold more important when spread betting.

Let's consider the case where Bob, from the previous example, decides to place a £10 buy spread bet instead of buying the shares. He buys for £10 a point, as £10 "isn't very much", and if the shares get to 700 (easily possible he reckons) then he'll make around £1000, which would be "very handy".

And we'll assume he trades the same way he did with the shares – in other words, he holds the bet open while the shares fall all the way to 24p. And, again, at every stage of the share price falling he has an excuse why the market is wrong and why the shares will bounce back (i.e. an excuse for why he is not wrong).

If Bob bought the bet at 603 and still held it at 24 he would sustain a loss of £5790 (£10 x 579).

£5790!

- And this was only a £10 a point bet!

- And this was a FTSE 100 company!

- And he was only looking to make a £1000 profit in the first place!

Frankly, you're not going to last long in the market with a forecast profit/loss profile like this:

- Upside = £1000

- Downside = £5790

> The lesson is: when spread betting it is essential to use stop losses to impose discipline and limit losses.

So, stops are used a lot in spread betting because **you can lose so much more than your initial stake**. Indeed, some spread firms open one up for you automatically when you place your bet (which you can then change).

Most spread bettors use stops – they are a protection against losing too much on any one trade. With a stop loss in place, in most situations you know the maximum loss you are likely to make on a particular trade.

Stop loss examples

Let's look at some examples of using stops.

Long share bet

You decide you like a share and it's 500p to buy. You decide to place a spread bet at £10 a point. Remember, this gives you a total exposure of £5000 (£10 x 500) – in other words, if the company went bust you'd owe the spread betting company £5000.

However, the maximum loss you are prepared to take is £500.

The question is then: if the share price starts falling, at what price do you need to sell it to limit your loss to £500?

The calculation is straightforward: you have placed a bet at £10 a point, so a fall of 50p will result in a loss of £500 (£10 x 50).

So, you need to set a stop-loss order with the trigger at 450 (500 - 50).

If the price hits 450, your position is closed and the £500 loss is auto booked by the spread-firm's computer.

Short share bet

Stops can be used to protect short, as well as long, positions.

You decide to go short of a company (i.e. bet on it going down in price).

This company is also at 500p and you bet £10 a point. Remember: as you short:

- you **make** money if the price *falls*, and

- you **lose** money if the price *rises*.

So your stop loss has to be *higher* than your entry price.

You still don't want to lose more than £500 (which, remember, is the equivalent of 50 points).

So your stop should be set at 550p (500 + 50).

Short index bet

Now let's imagine you felt the FTSE 100 had gone too high and a sell-off was due. So you short the index at 5500.

Putting on the stop is exactly the same as with a share.

You decide the maximum loss you want to take is 50 points, so your stop loss would be at 5550. However, as discussed elsewhere in the book, because the FTSE moves so fast a 50p stop might be too tight – you may want to put on a lower stake and a higher stop.

> With most spread-bet firms you can put on your stop as you place the trade, simply find the 'stop loss' or 'order' button and type in your stop (trigger) price.

Amending a stop

Long Aggreko bet

Let's go back to the Aggreko example.

Assume you decided Aggreko was a good bet, so you bought £10 a point at 552. Let's say that your spread betting firm puts on a stop loss automatically for you at 520. At this level you now know your maximum loss is:

```
552 - 520 = 32 points

32 points x £10 per point = £320
```

However, you may think that Aggreko is very volatile so you want to place the stop lower. In other words, you want your stop loss to be triggered when the share is definitely on the way down, but not when the share price is merely fluctuating up and down a bit.

One option is to set the stop loss 10% below the current price (of 552), which would put it at roughly 500.

> Personally, I always set a stop away from a whole number.

So I would go for 490, giving me a maximum loss of £620 (552 - 490 x £10).

Going lower stops me getting 'spiked out' by a quick spike down, although I take the risk of losing more money. It's a personal thing and you have to make your decisions circumspectly as you get more experienced.

It's easy to change a stop loss. Normally, you just press 'order' or 'stop loss', and then amend the stop loss to where you want it to be. Now, say Aggreko goes your way and whizzes up to 600, you could now amend the stop to 552. At which point your downside is set to be zero (if the price subsequently falls, you will sell at 552, which was your buy price). So, you then can't lose on this trade!

This is called using a trailing stop – I will talk more about this on page 72.

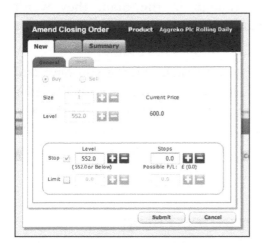

Amending a stop loss on Tradefair

Tradefair uses auto stops when you place a bet, so do check the level and change it to the one you want. IG, on the other hand, asks you to type your criteria into the stop-loss box. It all depends on the firm but it's easy enough once you are used to a certain company.

Alternatively, place your own stop loss at the start!

Let's look at the Aggreko trade box on Tradefair. You can see that just underneath where you put in the pounds per point is a box for a stop. Simply place your stop loss in that box.

Tradefair, Aggreko, adding your own stop loss when placing a bet

And it's the same with IG, although in the main they won't automatically give you a stop loss so you need to remember to type one in if you choose to use stops.

Generally you should be able to go into each holding you have and amend its stop loss either higher or lower. For example, with Tradefair you click 'order book', click on the share, and then change the stop loss, remembering to press 'amend' or 'done' at the end. You should then get an email confirming the change and see the new stop under 'open orders'.

Standard stop vs. guaranteed stop

One thing to point out (just when your head is already spinning, eh?) is that there are two different types of stops:

- standard

- guaranteed.

1. Standard stops

Let's say you own some shares that are currently trading at 52p, and you have placed a stop-loss order at 48p. This means that if the share price falls to 48p, your stop order is triggered to sell the shares. But, here is the important question –

Note: I refer to trading shares in this explanation, but exactly the same applies for spread betting.

At what price are the shares actually sold?

Well, you might reasonably reply, at 48p, because that is where the stop order is placed.

However, this may not always be the case. If the market falls very quickly, liquidity in the shares could dry up, and the price could fall through the 48p level without any shares actually trading at that price. When prices fall, there's no law saying that the price must reduce in an orderly fashion like: 51, 50, 49, 48, 47...

It may be that the shares are trading at 52p, when bad news comes out and the shares slip to 50p, and then panic sets in, everyone tries to sell, there are no buyers, and the price drops straight to 43p!

If this happened, what would happen to the stop order?

Well, firstly, the stop loss would not have been triggered at 48p, because there was no trade at that level. When the first trade occurred below 48p, at 43p, then that would have triggered the stop, and the order to sell would have been placed into the market at that stage. The actual selling price therefore might be 43p – or lower if the market was continuing to fall quickly.

An alternative scenario would be for the price to fall and to trade at 48p (which would trigger the stop-loss order); however, because the market was falling so quickly (and on little volume) it may be that the shares end up being sold at a lower price.

> The key thing to remember is that if you place a stop-loss order at 48p you don't know exactly what price your shares will be sold at. You may hope it will be at the stop price – but there's no guarantee.

Liquidity

An important factor here is liquidity (the volume of shares that trade in a company). Big companies (e.g. Vodafone), whose shares enjoy high turnover (i.e. good liquidity), will generally suffer less from violent moves that can prove a problem for stop orders. The problem is more likely to occur with small companies, whose shares have low turnover (i.e. poor liquidity), where prices can move quickly with few shares actually trading.

However, even trading large shares does not always guarantee good liquidity in which stops can be executed at any price – which we will now look at.

Gapping at the open

Share markets are not open continuously – they have to close in the evenings to allow traders to go out, get drunk and go to lap dancing clubs. But while share markets are closed, the world doesn't stop, news is still coming out that can affect share prices. The result is that when markets open again on the following trading day, share prices can move quickly to react to events that happened when the markets were closed.

And the prices can move so quickly that no trades occur between the closing price of one session and the opening price of the following session.

Let's look at an example.

The following chart shows the price of RBS (I haven't got it in for RBS, but they are a very useful case study. OK, well, perhaps I have got it in for them … what a useless bunch of wallies.)

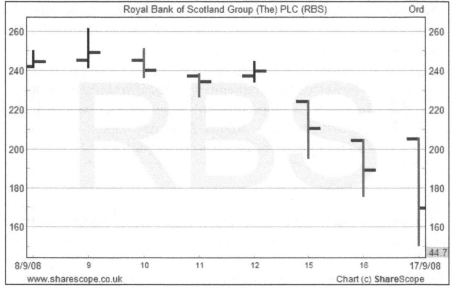

Example of gapping at the open (RBS)

On 12 September 2008 the shares closed at 239.75. This was a Friday, so there was a whole weekend of news for investors to ruminate on before the market opened again. On Monday morning, 15 September, the shares opened at 224p and then fell from there. There was no trade at all between the closing price of 239.75 (on Friday) and the opening price of 224 on Monday morning; the first price traded on Monday morning was 224p.

If an investor had placed a stop-loss order for the shares at 237p, the order would have been triggered as soon as that first trade of 224p went through on Monday morning, and the share would have been sold at 224 – *at best* (if the market was falling quickly, the shares may have ended up being sold for less).

Hmm, you may be thinking, these stop orders sound OK in theory, but they seem to fail just when you need them most! You may think that, and you wouldn't be very wrong.

However, there is a solution: guaranteed stops.

2. Guaranteed stops

Some brokers offer a *guaranteed* stop-loss order, which guarantees (hence the name – they're not fools these City types…) that the order will be transacted at exactly the same level as the stop trigger.

So, if you place a guaranteed stop-loss order at, say, 50p, and the price falls through that price, then you will sell out at 50p – regardless of what the liquidity was like at the time (i.e. regardless of whether there were actually any trades at 50p).

However, this feature does not come without a price – when you open the bet you get charged extra spread!

In general I don't use guaranteed stops as, over time, the extra spread cost cancels out the occasional benefits of definitely getting out. It might be worth it, though, if there is a very good reason. Say you were short of a share that had been bid for in the past, and you were worried a bid might knock your short to smithereens.

As a quick example let's use Aggreko again.

Say the spread price for Aggreko is 550-552. So, if you want to buy it, you would pay 552. However, if you wanted to place a guaranteed stop (let's say at 530p), then you might pay 554 to open the bet (instead of 552).

You would, in effect, be paying a premium for an insurance policy.

Do spread firms deliberately trigger stops?

A lot of spread bettors think the spread firms deliberately stop them out too early. Having visited some firms, on the whole I don't think this is true (see what I make of it in the later chapter where I take you on a visit to them). However, other market participants might try and trigger stops.

BUT, beware if your stop is too tight or too close to your entry price. And beware...

...the 8am stop-out!

What am I on about?

At 8am, as the market opens, spreads on shares can be wider than they would normally be because buyers and sellers haven't got their orders on yet. So, for example, a share that normally might be priced at 106-107 could be showing 102-108 at 8am, which quite quickly will right itself to 106-107 by, say, 8.05.

This happens on lots of shares.

And believe me, many spread bettors will switch on their machines at 8.10am to find an email telling them their position has been closed at a loss.

Why?

Because the spread-firm's computer will have been updated with the wide spread, noted the sell price, matched that with your stop loss – and bang! Your bet is a gonner.

This is despite the fact that no one would have traded at the silly wide spread right at the opening. But that doesn't stop you being taken out by the spread firm.

 This is why you should NEVER EVER have a stop that is too close to your entry price. You will keep getting stopped out and lose.

The above example is real and happened to me.

My stop to sell the share was at 102. The share had been trading at 106-107 for days and indeed when I saw it trading at 106-107 at 8.05 I never dreamed a few minutes later that an email would arrive telling me I had been stopped out at 102!

How could this happen?

I checked the chart and the trades for the day. Nope, no trades at below 106. The day chart showed it as not being below 106 for the day. BUT for about 60 seconds at the start of the day as the share was about to be traded I saw it had been 102-108. No one could have traded it. It wasn't a real price. So I called the spread-bet firm. I said I understood why it had been closed out but that it was unfair because it was never the real price or a proper traded price. The dealer then said something that you *must* be aware of:

❝ *It doesn't matter that the price at that time wasn't tradable. This was our price at the time taken from the market.* **❞**

This statement is really important. It reiterates the fact that you are playing against a bookie. You are playing the *bookie's price* and not what is really happening in the market.

It doesn't matter that in the real world the price of 102 never really existed in a real, tradable way. The price was there for a few seconds in print and that's that.

The moral of the story is: my stop should have been at around 98 not 102, to ensure that this didn't happen. Indeed, I went back into that share at 107 and placed the stop at 96 to be on the safe side.

Another moral of the story is:

 Check your stops in the market at the end of every day.

Are any of your stops too close to the current price so that if the share had a wide spread at 8am for a few seconds you might get taken out? If so, ensure you lower them before the start of the next day's trading.

It can be a good idea not to set them at whole numbers because market participants like to take out whole numbers. So set at 96 and not 100, 196 and not 200 etc.

Stop loss summary

- Remember to place your stop loss at the same time as your bet.

- If your spread firm has auto placed one for you, amend it if necessary.

- An ordinary (standard) stop loss will not necessarily sell out at the stop price.

- A guaranteed stop will always be implemented at the stop set price but costs you more spread.

- Beware the 8am stop-out!

Stop-loss and Target Setting

In this section we're going to look at:

1. stop-loss levels – where to set the trigger level for stop orders

2. targets – where to set the target level to take profits

1. Stop-loss levels

So now we're happy with the idea of stops, the big question is – *what's the best way to set a stop loss and a target price?*

Ah, if only there was a definitive answer, a magic formula – take the share price, divide by two, multiply by 30, then add 10 and minus the square root of the answer, whilst standing on your head and reciting the alphabet backwards.

Sadly, in practice, it is an inexact science.

It partly depends on the amount you have in your account, partly depends on the amount you are willing to lose; and it depends on the volatility of the share.

Remember, indices are *very* volatile. Place a bet on the Dow and it could move 200 points either way within a couple of hours, wiping out a stop wherever you put it. Mining shares are often crazily volatile too, as are some FTSE 100 stocks.

Regarding at what level to place a stop, I have a kind of rule of thumb. I start at 10% (away from the current price) and then tweak it from there, depending on where punters have bought and sold it in the past.

Best to have an example, eh?

Stop target examples

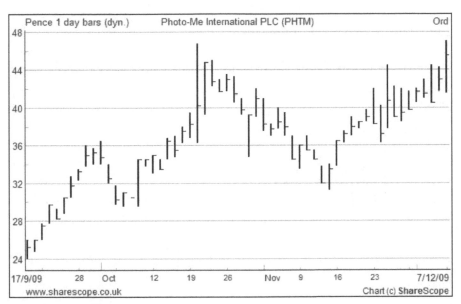

Photo-Me (PHTM)

I bought Photo-Me at 34p in early November 09.

Now, what about the stop loss?

First, the 10% rule of thumb would place the stop at around 30.5 (34 - 3.5).

Then I look at the chart and see the last time it bounced after going down was at 30! So I lower the stop a bit further, to go under that at 28. The reason is that history often repeats itself. It bounced before at 30 so it could easily do it again. Therefore I don't want to go with the 30.5 in case I get stopped out at the 30p level (after which it could bounce and rise again).

After I had entered the trade and placed my stop at 28, the share then rose before falling back to close at 30. Placing my stop at 28 (under 30!) meant it was not quite activated. A lucky escape, as the price then did rise – and carried on rising very nicely through November. Any tighter and I would have been stopped out at a small loss, and the stop order wouldn't really have been helping me at all.

Let's look at another example.

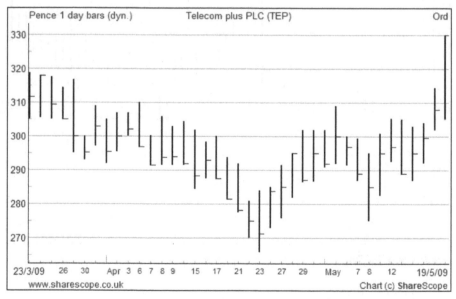

Telecom Plus (TEP)

I bought Telecom Plus in May 09 at 300.

10% of that is 30p, so I put my stop at 270. But look at the chart – it bounced right off 270 before back in April. (Called "support" in jargon). With a wide spread I want to lower the stop a little just to be sure, and I go for 260.

See what I mean? Have a look back in time, check where the price bounced before, and set your stop a little below that price. In other words, set your stop just a bit lower from where everyone else might be setting their stops. Then you have less of a chance of being bounced out.

Note: the challenge when setting a stop is to set a level that will be activated when the share makes a decisive move, but is not activated on a small, insignificant move (that is often quickly reversed).

Obviously this is just what I do, and you might want to design your own methods for setting a stop loss.

Don't forget the 8am stop-out

One thing to remind you of again is the 8am stop-out.

Let's say your share is currently 500 and your stop is 490. At 8am there is every chance that for a few seconds the share could open up at 490-510 before quickly settling at 499-501, where it should be. Yet your stop will have taken you out.

So on stocks valued between, say, 400 and 800, I ensure my stop is at least 20 points below the current price overnight.

Now targets…

2. Targets

The question here is – *where to set the target price where you are happy to take profits?*

My default position is to set a target of 20%. After all, why buy something unless you can get at least 15% plus on it?

Let's have a look again at that Photo-Me example.

My default of 20% would set the target here of about 41p (34p + 20%).

The chart tells us very little here because it hasn't reached a peak of 41p for so long, it's not possible to decide what to do with much reference to the past. So I'd stick with my 20% (41p), but I would ensure the stop loss rose under the price by about 3p if it went on rising.

The Telecom Plus target is a lot easier. Default 20%, which is 360 – now, a quick look at the chart shows it has peaked a few times around 360, so 360 it is! No need to change.

Sometimes a share does so well it goes through a target and keeps on going. In which case, I stick with it even if it's for a longer period than you might expect with a spread bet.

I bought Microgen (MCGN) at 45p in March 09, setting a stop loss of 41 and a target of 53.

Microgen (MCGN)

It went through the 53p target pretty quickly. So, I raised the stop on the initial buy and bought some more at 54.

Then some more at 65.

I still hold it at 85p, with stops on at 70, and 75. Big profits will just be locked in now if the price goes down a lot. And if it continues up, I'll raise the stops.

Stop losses vs. targets

An important point here:

 Stop losses should be far tighter than targets.

If you set both stops and targets at 10% you would need an awful lot more winners than losers to win overall. But with 10% stops and 20% targets you can take more losses than winners but still win overall.

This is an important point – think about that for a bit. In fact, I'll repeat it – *you can take more losses than winners but still win overall*

 Never ever be afraid of taking a small loss.

The other point is that a 20% target could be your initial target and, if you can, you may want to run them to more than 20% – in fact, one or two big winners can easily cover lots of small losses. However, you should decide on your target *before* you place the trade and don't let emotions rule once the price starts to move.

Trailing Stop Losses/Raising Stops

More on stop losses?

Yep. But we've nearly finished on these and this bit coming is really interesting – so listen up.

Let's look first at a standard stop loss.

Say you buy a share at 55p and place a stop loss at 45p. And then, over the following few days, the shares soar to 110p. Whoopee!

But then the share price turns round, and falls down to 35p. Not so whoopee.

You have saved some money – your stop got you out at 45p – but that is small compensation when all you can think of is that lost profit.

But there is a solution: trailing stops!

This is how it works.

In the above example, when you bought the shares at 55p, you would have placed a trailing stop loss of 10p. (Many spread firms will do these.)

This means that, initially, the stop would be placed at 45p (55-10) – just as in the first case. However, when the shares start moving up, the stop loss is adjusted upwards as well. So, that, when the share price hit 70p and then fell back a few pence, the stop is adjusted to 60p (70-10); when the share price then climbs higher to, say, 88p and then falls back a few pence, the stop loss is adjusted to 78p (88-10). And, finally, when the share price hits a high of 110p the stop loss is set at 100p – and so this is the price you sell at, while the share price falls back to 35p.

Pretty neat, eh?

The idea really is to lock in profits – and to lock them in unemotionally. What I mean by that is that you set the stop loss beforehand and if the price hits the stop target, you sell automatically, you don't think,

> 'Hmm, well that's no good, however this just looks like a temporary correction, the chart doesn't look too bad [if you squint your eyes and hold it slightly sideways], no I think I'll hold on a bit and wait for the price to bounce back...'

Automatic or manual?

There are two ways of implementing trailing stops:

1. Your spread betting firm does it for you automatically. This can be a very useful service, but not all spread betting firms offer this so you need to check if yours does.

2. You do it manually yourself. In this case, as a price rises you occasionally move up the stop loss underneath it. The danger with this approach is that you may forget to adjust the stop.

For example, you've bought Aggreko at 552p and it's reached 700 – and a marvellous (paper) profit but you're not sure whether to take it. Well, just raise your stop loss to, say, 670. If Aggreko carries on going up, you can carry on raising it – if Aggreko starts to slip, your profit is taken.

I think trailing stops are a great idea and you ought to look into using them.

Here's an example of how I used one on a FTSE bet.

Trailing stop example

I bought the FTSE at 5104 for a fiver a point. Two days later the index had risen to 5304, giving me a profit of £1000. I wasn't sure whether to take the profit or not. So I decided to keep the position open, whilst raising my stop to 5270. The FTSE carried on up a bit but then fell heavily. While I was out getting a coffee, my stop got me out and I still took a handsome £850 profit – if I hadn't raised the stop, the profits would have been way lower.

(We will look at stops from the spread betting firms' point of view in the visit-to-spread-firms chapter later on.)

Target/stop summary

- Set lower stops and higher targets, for example, 10% and 20% respectively.

- Don't set stops too close to the entry price.

- Beware 8am stop-outs – check your stops every evening and amend if need be.

- Set stops a little below support, and targets a little below resistance.

5. What Markets Should You Trade?

Top Traded Markets

This table lists the top traded markets for spread bettors.

Brent Crude	Usually quoted for the next month so check the expiry date. It has a tight spread – something like say 70.65 to 70.70 – and moves fast!
FTSE 100 rolling	Nice tight spread.
Gold rolling	Often countercyclical to the main market, and hey, as you don't buy physical gold, you don't even need to stick the bars under the bed!
S&P 500 rolling	The top 500 companies in the US in one index.
Dow Jones	The top 30 US companies and it moves like lightning. A £5-a-point bet is a massive bet. It has been known to move 700 points in one day.
EUR/USD	Euro vs. US dollar.
GBP/USD	Sterling vs. US dollar. Very tight spread, check your stake.
Barclays	The most popular traded stock.
Microsoft	When trading US stocks, remember they are quoted in dollars!
Rio Tinto	The biggest mining stock and one of the most popular day trades.

As you can see, quite a range: commodities, currencies, equity indices and individual equities.

But every market is different and I would suggest that, before tackling these big markets, you understand what you're doing, get the stake right, and have a trade plan.

> I don't trade commodities or currencies so I can't help you much with those, but if that's the kind of thing you fancy, there are a lot of books that can. If you go to my website and press 'books', you can search for these types of publications.

In this section we're going to look primarily at individual equities and equity indices (and there's a brief note on commodities at the end).

First, individual equities...

Shares

Personally, I trade pretty much everything from FTSE shares to small caps and occasionally the indices too. I'm assuming you've already done some standard share trading or investing in your normal stockbroking account, so why not simply start by trading the shares you are used to?

Say, for example, you have a longer-term hold in your portfolio that you bought at 200 and which is now at 250. You expect it to go higher, but maybe you had no cash left inside your ISA (a great tax-free way to invest). You can take a spread bet! Think of it as a shorter-term play to add some more to a share you like. If all goes well, you can sell it a bit higher and bank some extra profits.

An alternative could be: you bought the shares at 200, they're now 250. You think they will go still higher but short-term there is a market downturn. You can "hedge" your open profits by short-term shorting them with spread betting. You don't need to sell your shares and buy them back later with all the costs involved. Your short in the shares will cover the short-term downside.

Note: do be careful on the volatility of shares (i.e. how much, and how quickly, thay can move up or down). Volatility that can be uncomfortable for a share trader can be catastrophic for a spread bettor if they have leveraged their bets by using all the margin available.

FTSE 100 shares

FTSE shares often move in tandem with the general market. And, given that the UK market is heavily influenced by the US market, if the Dow Jones closed down the previous evening, chances are your favoured share will head downwards too and open up lower in the morning.

These and other short-term influences you have no control over.

You have to expect these shares to move extremely rapidly. Between 2007 and 2010, most FTSE shares went up and down faster than a bungie-jumping Mr Blobby. Therefore, be careful when setting stop losses. Make sure that they're not too close to your opening price or you could find yourself stopped out all the time. Be careful around 1.30pm and 3pm; FTSE shares can get very volatile when economic stats are reported at these times from the US.

FTSE shares can also move sharply for crazy reasons beyond any control or expectation. For example, when Dubai said it might default on its debt, shares fell alarmingly for two days before coming right back. Or when Greece said it was in deep hummus. Or whenever someone important in the US says something bad about the economy.

Mining shares

Mining shares generally move in line with the underlying commodity markets. But it must be said that FTSE mining shares, such as Rio Tinto, are crazy. In fact, mining shares are *the* craziest. You need a hard hat to be trading these – and for beginners I would say leave well alone. I wouldn't be digging up trades here personally.

FTSE 250 shares

These are the next 250 companies in terms of size listed on the London Stock Exchange after the top 100 companies in the FTSE 100 Index. They don't move quite as fast as the FTSE shares, meandering along a lot more slowly. Personally I prefer trading these in the main.

One thing to watch for, though: bigger spreads mean that at 8am spreads can be wide, and it's often best to avoid dealing in them too early in the day. Also, be careful with stops, as a wide spread at the beginning of the day could knock you out. However, with the FTSE 250 you can choose wisely and pick companies with great prospects – or ones with bad prospects, if you want to short.

Small cap shares

Small cap shares go up to a market capitalisation of around £300m, FTSE 250 shares then go to a cap of about £1.3bn, and after that we are talking FTSE 100 levels.

Small cap shares move the most slowly, and sometimes not at all!

There is nothing wrong with buying small cap shares with a spread bet but whatever you do, do NOT overdo it. That's because small cap shares are often not very liquid. If you build a big position, and want to sell the lot quickly, you may have problems.

This is not the spread firm's fault. It will have to deal with market makers who only, by the rules, have to sell a relatively small amount of the shares at the price offered on the screen. So check out the size of trade that is normal in the share (rule of thumb for small caps is about £5000 worth)... or check Level II, if you have it (see p.128 if you're unsure what this is).

For example, say you bought a small cap stock at 50p for £50 a point. No problem, as the average size the market makers deal in, you discover, is 5000 shares, the same as £50 a point.

IG probably has the best coverage of the small cap companies.

A good rule of thumb is to have a toe in all these markets. You may want one or two FTSE 100 shares for a bit of volatility to short-term trade, some FTSE 250 to hold for a bit longer and which presents less of a headache as they don't move so fast, and some small cap companies you think could be future winners.

Indices

Say you decide the markets have had a good ride and you think they're going to fall, what better way of making money than by betting on something like the FTSE 100 to drop? Or if the market has tanked, and you think a rise is due, what better way to act than by buying the FTSE?

Note: when I refer to the "FTSE" I mean the FTSE 100 Index. There are other indices, for example FTSE 250 of mid-size companies, but for the moment I'll be focusing on the FTSE 100 (which is also sometimes called the *footsie*).

Let's take a look.

The FTSE has risen all the way to 5000 from 3600 and you think it is ripe for a fall. So type FTSE into the search engine of your spread firm.

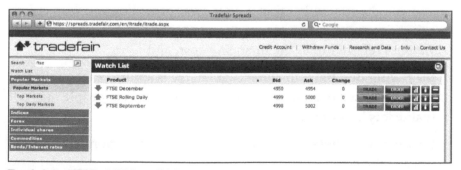

Tradefair, FTSE, 3600 to 5000

As you can see, you have the choice of:

- **FTSE rolling** at one point spread (4999-5000) or

- **FTSE September** at 4998-5002 or

- **FTSE December** at 4950-4954.

FTSE rolling is only a 1-point spread (that is a Good Thing) – you will get charged a very small amount to keep it open every day.

FTSE quarterlies (March, June, September, December) expire at four points throughout the year (usually the third Friday of these months at about 10am) – you may have to manually 'roll over' your bets if you want to hold the position open for a long time. For example, if you buy the March bet in February, but want to hold the bet open to May, then when the March bet expires you will have to close the March bet and open a new bet in the June bet.

Some firms even quote monthly bets. In the example above, the December quote is much lower than the rolling quote because things like ex-dividends are taken into account in the price.

Financing costs

One thing to note is that the quarterly prices can be very different to the current price. For instance, say it is currently August: the September quote is similar to the rolling quote, as the September quote closes in just three weeks' time. But the December price is quite different, with a wider spread.

The reason for this is as follows. As mentioned before, when you trade on margin, the spread-bet firm is effectively providing you with credit, but there is – not surprisingly – a charge for that credit. This charge is sometimes referred to as the financing cost, and –

- for **rolling day bets**: the financing charge is applied each night that the bet is rolled over (it is usually so small that some people may not realise it is happening),

- for **quarterly bets**: the financing charge is incorporated into the price of the bet.

So, a quarterly bet may have a higher price than a rolling day bet, not because the spread bet firm thinks the market is going up, but the quarterly price reflects the financing charge. And the financing charge of a quarterly will necessarily be very different from accumulated overnight charges on the rolling day bets. In other words, it is wrong to think of the rolling day bets as "cheaper".

> When spread betting was first introduced it was primarily aimed at City traders who were used to the idea of the financing costs of long-dated bets. But when spread-bet firms started marketing increasingly to ordinary people, they found that many didn't understand why the prices on the long-dated bets were so different from the current price – and so they introduced rolling day bets which got over the problem.

Stake size

Be careful with your staking; remember the FTSE can move 100 points easily in *one day*. Therefore if you have a £10 a point bet and the FTSE moves the wrong way you could be down £1000 just like that! Even a £5 a point is quite a big bet. Generally, unless you have deep pockets, be a bit wary and look at £2 to £3 a bet.

Up or down?

To place an up bet, remember to press 'buy' or press the up arrow; and to go short, press the 'sell', or the down arrow.

Make certain you are pressing the right button.

This may sound obvious, but we've all – including the top traders – made mistakes and bought when we meant to sell.

Fat finger trades

 Beware – it is so easy to push the wrong button and put on a much bigger stake than you thought!

I've done it myself. At a seminar I decided to place – live in front of a lot of people – a £10 per point short-term FTSE trade. I pressed 0 one too many times and before I knew it I had bet £100 a point! A crazily high stake. Of course it gave everyone a laugh, but at home I could easily have missed the extra 0, gone out and found myself £5k down if the FTSE had moved 50 points!

'Fat finger' trades, as these are called, are well known, and big traders have often moved markets by mistakenly pressing the wrong buttons!

One of my readers recounts:

> **66** Don't twitch while spread betting – I literally touched the buy button by accident while I was using a deal ticket to calculate deposit requirements etc. Fortunately the result was a small gain as I just exited shaking, asap. That 15-second countdown for deciding on an ordinary purchase of shares is now so reassuring! **99**

Exactly! With a normal trade you normally get 15 seconds to check your trade; with a spread bet it happens in a blink. Don't twitch. And always double check if you're putting on a trade after drinking a lot of coffee!

...and stops

Remember to be careful with stops. If you set your stop just 40 points away from the current FTSE level, or something like that, you could get spiked out! Think very hard about where to place it. I look on it as insurance and often place it 200 points away and decide when to exit manually.

The FTSE and other indices generally trade 24 hours, except at weekends, so it is possible to get stopped out overnight.

It's very easy to trade an index like the FTSE, but should you?

Well, perhaps this is best summed up by a conversation I had with a trader about people who trade indices.

"How many people lose?" I asked.

"Nearly everyone," he replied.

Does that answer the question!

Now, I have, over time, won at indices – but I trade them selectively and certainly not every day, or even every week.

If you are starting out, be cautious – especially when it comes to staking. Remember what I said. £5 a point seems low, but it isn't!

Hedging my longs

I tend to be more of a shorter of the FTSE, because I like the idea of hedging my longs if the FTSE appears to be in a shorter-term decline. ["Hedging my longs" – is that like pruning your underwear? – Ed]

Oh yes, sorry, jargon alert: what do I mean by "hedging my longs"?

It means that, generally, outside of my spread betting I'll probably have mainly share holdings with a stockbroker. If the FTSE 100 goes down it's likely that some of those shares will fall in price as well. But selling all the shares would be fiddly and also costly. It would be a hassle, especially if I think the market will bounce back shortly. So, instead of selling shares all I have to do is spread bet the FTSE short to offset (or hedge) the fall.

If the FTSE falls, then I make money from it with my short bet, which covers some of the falls that might happen to my shares. Once the FTSE stops falling I can bank the profit, my shares will go back up and I'll have weathered the storm.

I have made some nice, in fact some very big, sums shorting the FTSE – often keeping the bet open for a few weeks. One example was during the bear market decline from 6800 to 3600 in 2007-8.

Let's have a look at that fall and the bounce back up to 5300.

FTSE 2007-8, fall from 6800 to 3600 and rise to 5300 (2006-2010)

As you can see, once the index gets into an up or a down move it can stay there for some time. And so, if the trend continues, it can be worth sticking with a FTSE bet for a while, rather than just the short term.

A small proportion of day traders do manage to short-term bet the FTSE and make money, but it is very easy to lose money. The main thing is: if you get the trend wrong, *get out fast* – ensure you don't start taking big losses.

Don't be stubborn

For example, one tipster in an investment magazine shorted the FTSE when it got back to 4000, but stuck to his guns for months while it rose and rose … and rose. Eventually he caved in when it got back to 5000. But he waited 1000 points! That should never happen. Just because you think the economy is screwed up doesn't necessarily mean the markets will move down. Markets undershoot and overshoot far longer than you can remain solvent going against the trend.

Coming a cropper

I have included one or two stories in the Traders' Tales section about coming a cropper playing indices but here's one that literally popped into my mailbox as I wrote this section.

" I wouldn't ask but [I've] never been in such a mess before.

Basically, I took a long-term view on a few major indices and used a strategy of 12-week breakout etc. but now they have all gone sour. I have not stopped them out but decided to hedge them all instead...I feel a little nuts as I have the following open –

Austalia 200: £2/pt, Long

FTSE 100: £2.22/pt, Long

Dax: £2.22/pt, Long

Nasdaq: 5.22/pt, Long

Dow: £1/pt, Long

Dow: £5.9/pt, Short (as the hedge)

What I am wondering is...now that I am holding losses in the thousands and have stabilised them with the Dow hedge...at what point do you take your profit from your FTSE hedges? Do you wait for a turnaround being visible or start cutting and balancing where you could...? "

Oh boy! I had to write back to him with a huge bollocking. He really ought to close everything down to get out of this silly mess he's in. Worse, he now has something like £100k exposure to the markets and I bet, judging by some extra comments he made, he doesn't have more than £10k in the bank.

He needs to close out and spend time reading up on risk and money management and only come back to index trading when he is sure that he knows how to run his trading positions with proper risk management in place.

Be warned: this is the type of terrible mess you can get into by spread betting indices. It's also clear that this chap simply started gambling and betting beyond his means.

It's hard work

My view is that it is possible to trade indices profitably but most people fail. I think the traders that succeed work very hard at it and in the most part concentrate on just trading one index and nothing much else.

Most use technical analysis of some sort – if you want to get into it then check my website for decent books to buy in this area – but do think about specialising in it. You will need to.

Looking around at the various bulletin boards that discuss trading the FTSE, it's easy to see beneath the bravado of some posters that they've actually lost money. And that has happened time after time.

So, in my opinion, don't discount-deal in the FTSE or other indices – but if you do get into it, do so slowly and by risking only small stakes.

This is a good place to look at a FTSE trading story from a reader:

> **"** After about 6 months of running a player account, I decided to take the plunge and run a real account. I've mostly been day trading the FTSE 100 based on what's being reported in the business news and with the aid of some charting software, namely MACD and RSI. Everything went pretty well for a number of weeks, and I was about £400 up on my original float at one point.
>
> The best day was the 24th of September where I shorted at £5 a point to make £310.
>
> Now my float is only about £4 up! Volatility seems to have been my undoing as I never allow a trade to get more than about £70 in the red. I do run very tight stop losses to avoid getting wiped out. Ironically, at the end of each day of frustrating trading, the index is mostly at the level I expected it to be from the start.
>
> Any advice would be welcome. I know you don't trade the FTSE often – perhaps like me you find the volatility too difficult to cope with. I'm planning to go back to the player account for a while to avoid any more losses. I'll drop the bets down to £1 a point as well to see if that will help me ride the bumps better, and stop me closing out bets too early. **"**

The problem here is the reader is *just* dealing in the FTSE. Its volatility is indeed significant, so such a dependency is liable to play havoc with you. It has nourished an obsession, and led him to just break even after a lot of work. If you play the FTSE, do it as a side dish and not the main course.

Opening times

Spread-bet markets mainly open up just after 8am and close just before 4.30pm. But on some markets you can trade 24 hours a day if you really want to.

FTSE bets don't stop at 4.30pm (when the LSE stops trading) – you can carry on trading until at least 9pm online (when the Dow closes) and pretty much 24 hours (bar the weekend) by phone. The spread tends to trade wider after hours.

How does that work?

Well, the spread firms rely on the futures markets (to hedge many of the trades made by spread bettors) and this includes using the futures markets in the US, which stay open late into the European evening. This means you can close out your FTSE bet at 8pm at night if you want to. Although do be aware that spreads can widen after the underlying market (i.e. the LSE) closes.

Evening FTSE prices generally mirror whatever the Dow Jones is doing: if that is sinking, so will the FTSE price. In the evening (say 9pm) when the Dow closes, you will see that the current FTSE quote will often be very different to how the FTSE closed, and that tells you how the market may start the following day.

So don't try and be a clever clogs and think: "Oooh the Dow Jones closed a lot lower and the FTSE will fall tomorrow – I must go short!" The FTSE fall will already be factored into the price. Do you think the spread betting firms are stupid or wot?

Commodities

Commodities such as oil and gold are among the top traded markets – short-term traders love them as they are so volatile.

Oil is an interesting one. For example, say you have some oil shares in your portfolio. Those will tend to move with the oil price. Lets say it's a big oil stock, and you think that over the next three years it will move up, so it's a long-term hold, but you also think that the oil price is due to come down a bit in the short term.

Well, you could hold on to your shares but short the oil price – in other words, hedge your position! If you get it right your spread bet will make money, the oil share may come down a little but that's okay as it's a long-term hold. Rather than selling your share your oil-price short bet might make up the money that the share loses, or more. If you got it wrong, come out of the oil short quickly, take a small loss and remember that your shares will be going up!

 But do be aware that many commodity bets are crazily volatile. In my book, it's gambling, and I don't touch them.

6. I Visit Two Spread Betting Firms

Just for you, dear readers, I rose from the laziness of pushing a few buttons and drinking tea and eating toast all day to do some real research. Though I was also myself quite interested in what I might find.

I get many emails about spread betting firms, and a lot of conspiracy theories too. It's rare a day goes by when I don't get an email along the lines of:

❝ My SB [spread betting] firm has deliberately stopped me from making a profit on my trade. I lost a lot of money and it's the spread-firm's fault. ❞

It would seem, judging by how often I get this type of message, that most spread bettors, on realising a loss, prefer to blame the loss on *anyone* but themselves. I get the impression that people believe that spread betting firms are staffed with nasty blokes in pinstripe suits with bottles of gin by their side, deliberately trying to make them lose.

As in –

❝ *Ha ha!! Look – Brian's stop losses are nearly hit. Let's hit 'em anyway!!* ❞

Then they push the button and laugh themselves senseless – another sucker blown away.

So I wondered: are spread firms really out to get their punters? Are some of my readers right to blame the spread firms for their losses?

Given that most conspiracy theories are, well, how can I put this delicately – just a load of bollocks – I didn't think I'd find much. But it was worth trying. Also, I felt it would be interesting to see what really does happen at the other end of the process when the button on the web page is pressed to trade.

After all, I'd been spread trading for years and never really knew what happened at the other end. Do they just take all the bets and hope you lose? Do they cheer you on when you win? Or could they not care less either way?

Frankly, it takes a lot to get me out of the house and into people's offices. But I decided, in the interests of you, dear reader, that I would visit a couple of the firms – indeed, the two firms I use the most – to see for myself what goes on.

I just want you to understand the tribulations I had to go through to get this done. The Tube has NOT got any better since I last used it a long while back, in the days when I had to do more than put on my slippers to get to work. The carriages still smell of old farts, and wee wee, and they stop all the time in tunnels rather than at the stops. But I braved them and their wee (four times, there and back) for you. That's love.

We're talking real investigative journalism here, direct from the front-lines. Kate Adie – eat your heart out.

I visited Tradefair one week and IG the next.

Tradefair

Tradefair is the sister company to the huge and highly successful Betfair. The spread betting side of the sporting-markets giant is handled by London Capital Group, which is listed on the market and worth around £40 million.

Tradefair is in the City for real, in quite a nice office block, close to where City people really work. In fact, walking to the offices the people I passed were all pretty much youngish blokes in mid-range suits, their fingers holding cigarettes and stabbing Blackberries.

Despite the recession that had kicked in as I was writing this book (if you got this book from a bargain bucket for 10p in the year 2018, we're talking about the recession that started in 2007 and ended in 2009) they all looked pretty happy with their lot.

It's not a bad part of London, I guess.

Offices and staff

So, into the Tradefair office.

What are you expecting?

A massive place, full of aggressive blokes screaming at each other, "Sell!" "Buy!" "Quick – hit one of Brian's stops!" A load of sniggering schoolboys, with posh accents, going "Yah, yah, yah?" about the place? Loads of blokes jumping up and down and shouting into phones like you see on the telly?

Nope – you've got it all wrong. It's the opposite. Really quiet.

Where are the blokes in pinstripes?

I don't know, but not here, that's for sure.

In fact, it's mainly guys and girls in their 20s and 30s wearing smart casual gear (somewhere between Next and Ted Baker). And a surprising number of girls, in fact – the mix is nearly half and half.

The traders are all quiet, polite and look like they have fun. Or at least they aren't as terminally bored-looking as people in most offices I've been to. They seem to be engaged and enjoying the work, rather than sitting there emailing mates or updating their Facebook pages or Twattering. (Or maybe they just did that after I left!)

The coffee machine was rubbish, of course. And so I turned down any offers of what strange liquid might eventually gurgle forth from its depths. I was warned in advance so I had a Starbucks before I arrived! (I only like the good stuff.)

I was given full access to the trading desk, and sat next to one of the main dealers, Andy.

So what did I find out?

Everyone seems to have a different role; they generally seem to work in twos. So there are two working on the shares desk, two on the FTSE desk, two on FX, etc. I guess the main surprise is that the computer pretty much takes all the bets as they come in, and I could see the list of bets coming in:

Rolling FTSE sell — Vodafone buy — rolling FTSE buy — British Telecom sell — etc.

The majority are not that large; say a fiver a point. The most popular focus appears to be the rolling FTSE 100, which isn't surprising as Tradefair does a one-point spread when most of the firms do two. As the bets come in, those working on the specialist desks will check the company's exposure and take action if necessary.

Tradefair's business model, to me, seems … well, fair. Pretty much all the bets are taken by the computer as they come in, with extra spread added on to each bet (which of course is where all the spread firms can definitely make some money). The only bets that aren't automatically taken are those that are large – they will flash up and the dealer needs to check they can hedge that bet. Or, if someone is winning a lot of money, their bet might flash up, as it might need to be hedged right away.

Hedging

I can hear some of you cry – *"what does 'hedged' mean?"*

It just means the firm is buying or selling shares to offset the bet.

Let's take a share example.

The trader looking after the shares desk has a spreadsheet of all the quoted shares. The sheet tells him the company's exposure to each share, with the amounts clients are long or short of them. Each share has its own limit. Let's take a mid-range share. I don't think it's fair to reveal the exact numbers involved, but let's just say, for example, a reasonably popular share in the FTSE 250 might have a limit of £50,000. So, once the company is exposed to £50k's worth of bets on this share, the trader will buy its actual shares in the stock market.

Let's say the company is exposed to £100,000 of the share. Chances are now that if you put on a £5000 trade, they will buy the shares in the market. So they are going with your bet. Or hedging. If the share price then rises significantly, they will have to pay out to the traders who took out long bets, but they can afford to do that from the profits they've made with their positions in the underlying shares. In other words, their actions in the underlying shares are to cover their liabilities on the spread bets taken out by their clients.

If there are a lot of shorts on a share they might go in and sell the shares.

What are they trying to achieve by doing this?

A lot of the time they are just going with you, rather than against you, and pocketing the extra spread they charge. That means in essence they don't have to especially hope your bet will be a loser. It doesn't matter so much either way.

Tradefair also do some of the small cap shares. But they might limit these to, say, £30 a point per trade – because these are much harder to hedge. (Although you might be able to get away with more than one bet at 30.) Limits are generally much higher on FTSE 100 shares and you can usually put on as big a stake as you like (as long as you have the cash in your account!). And with index bets, really the sky is the limit (as long, again, as you have the money in your account). The index-trading desk operates in a similar way to the shares desk. Trades are taken and some are hedged.

I guess you could argue the dealers here are more risk managers than traders, ensuring the company will make money whatever trades are placed.

As with all spread-bet firms, remember: Tradefair gives you leverage. So, for example, if you wanted to trade Barclays and buy £5000-worth, you'd only need to have about £500 in your account. Don't forget what I've told you about the associated risks of this. If you have forgotten, go back and re-read it!

The dealer's view

Dealer Andy says –

❝ Most people lose, and the losers are more often than not the day traders. The more trades they put on, the more they seem to implode. The winners in this game tend to deal less and are very disciplined.

We do have a number of people who win over time, so it is possible with the right discipline and research. There is no getting away from the fact that it is not easy. In fact, even though I have been in the business for quite a while, I might make the same mistakes at home that clients do! ❞

The company is more than happy to have winning punters –

❝ For us a winning customer is no problem. We can simply place a buy in the market alongside their buy with us, sell when they sell, and pocket the extra spread which is our profit. They are happy, we are happy. And they will stay a customer for many years. This is much better in the end for us than a customer who loses quickly, decides spread betting is not for them and closes the account. ❞

Stops

Talking of losses, Tradefair sensibly imposes a stop loss on each trade – this means you know exactly the most you can lose when you open a position. Tradefair's computer will auto generate the stop loss but you can change it over time. This seems sensible to me, especially for newer traders.

I tackled Andy on what must be the most common complaint about spread-bet firms; in my best Jeremy Paxman voice –

❝ I'm always getting emails from people saying you stopped them out on purpose. ❞

Andy said –

❝ That is the most common complaint we get: 'You stopped me out!' The thing is, it isn't us, it's the market! ❞

Andy explained that the computer handles the stops – there really isn't someone sitting there doing it on purpose. Tick charts are used to decide if a stop is hit. "If a customer complains about being stopped out we are happy to mail them the tick chart," Andy says. Indeed, while

I was there a complaint came in by phone. The customer was immediately mailed the chart and was apparently fully satisfied.

Andy went on to say –

❝ We try hard to resolve people's complaints fairly. And if someone calls us we will look at it closely. It just isn't possible for us to watch people's accounts and try and stop them out manually, it would cost us more in staff than we'd get from any financial benefit! ❞

But the good news is, even if you are winning big money, your bets will still be allowed: unlike a sporting account with a bookie, you won't get closed down, promises Andy. Indeed, as I mentioned earlier, I believe that really is the case with all spread-bet firms; I have never heard of anyone having an account closed for making too much money. But it is nice to have it confirmed in person.

The busiest time for the trading desk at Tradefair is between 8am and 9am after the market has opened, then often at 1.30pm when the Americans tend to release market-moving data, and then again in the last hour or so after 3.30pm.

Talking about rolling spread bets, Andy agrees with me that – roughly speaking – rolling bets get more expensive after about two to three weeks: so if you generally hold bets for a reasonable period, it's worth going with the quarterlies.

I asked Andy how much people can win. "As much as they like," he says. "We had one client who went from £10,000 to £500,000 in two months and was doing really well..."

"Wow," I said, "500k – that *is* good going!"

"Yes," said Andy. "But he lost the lot within a few weeks!"

Why?

According to Andy, he lifted his stakes way too dramatically – so greed was his undoing. In fact, even though Andy can see where people go wrong with spread betting, he says he would find it hard to do it himself! According to Andy –

❝ I'm no different to clients and would struggle to do it myself. Mastering the discipline to spread bet can be difficult. People who lose just don't seem to go with the trends; they try to find the tops and bottoms of markets, and usually get wiped out in the attempt. They don't realise the size of their stakes and often put on far too big a bet for the amount of money they have. **"**

Wise words from Andy here – and some themes that you'll find discussed in other areas of this book.

So, all in all, I was pleasantly surprised with what I found. The business model looks fair for clients, and after my visit I remain happy to be a customer of Tradefair. It seems to me that their one-point daily FTSE spread is one of the main benefits of using them, and I think for newcomers to have a stop loss set up from the go is a good discipline to start with.

IG Index

The following week it was off to IG Index. It's the biggest spread betting firm, with a full stock-market listing and offices all over the world. As I write this book, the company is worth about £1.4bn, making it a potential FTSE 100 candidate in the future. It is expanding rapidly. It's called IG Group on the markets

Offices and staff

Its offices as I write are tucked away in a not so nice area, a bit away from the City (put it this way, there is no Starbucks close by, which is always a bad sign), but it's way bigger than Tradefair and has several floors. I guess not indulging in a plush location is a good sign for shareholders, though the reception has a very expensive-looking fish tank full of some very lovely fish. Highly relaxing (unless you just got stopped out on a duff bet). Fish, of course, make notoriously bad spread bettors – they just can't keep track of their trades.

The company is about to move office to Cannon Street.

Given IG is the market leader, with more client accounts than anyone else, the trading floor is a lot bigger than Tradefair's. It also runs some trading activities other than spread betting, such as CFDs (contracts for difference), and do a lot more real trading than Tradefair (so they have some proper trading desks as well).

Again, I had access to the spread betting area. But this time I agreed to try some coffee. If the coffee was a spread bet, it was a definite sell! However, in recompense I was given 50 IG pens and an IG baseball cap. I gave away the pens, but have still got the cap.

There are probably slightly fewer female traders at IG, but it's the same relaxed atmosphere as Tradefair (possibly even more so) and similar casual wear abounds (probably more at the Next end of the Next-Ted Baker spectrum). I think I upset head dealer Pete by suggesting his top was from Primark. "Fred Perry, actually," he said.

I'd say the staff here are a little older than at Tradefair, but then again the company has been going for a long time, and they all seem happy. Pete has been with IG for more than ten years; I reckon that is a pretty good sign. There are also plenty of other staff who've been here a long time. I have met dealers from one firm who didn't stay long because

they felt the firm were deliberately trying to stop their customers from winning. It doesn't happen at IG. (I can't tell you the company, as I have a general preference in life for not being sued.)

How they do business

Although IG's business model is pretty much the same as Tradefair's, Pete explains that really it is *volume* they are after. Simply put: the more bets they take, whether winning or losing for the client, the more profit they make.

As with Tradefair, there didn't seem to be any nasty blokes in dark glasses deliberately trying to stop customers out for a loss. Trades are in the main hedged (if you make a bet they make it too) especially the small caps. On putting the point that spread bettors often fear the spread firm deliberately wants to close them out or move a market to do so, Pete laughs –

66 We simply don't have the power to move a market in any share to stop clients out deliberately. Our systems do some automatic hedging for us. 99

There are a few differences between IG and Tradefair.

IG doesn't automatically set a stop loss – you can add it yourself, or not. It also does guaranteed stops and trailing stops (see elsewhere in the book for explanations of these chappies).

IG deals in more of the much smaller companies and has a massive range of shares on offer, even in tiddly companies. Pete explains –

66 We do allow bets on nearly every share up to the market size in that share, so on a very small company you may only be able to get a small spread bet on – but it's not our fault because that's all we could buy in the market ourselves to cover.

If one smaller share suddenly gets a lot of attention, maybe a newspaper tip, then we will only take bets by phone for a short time so we can cover the trades. We take as much business as we can on small caps, as long as we can trade it. Our aim really is to be a one-stop shop, so you should be able to buy or sell anything with us. 99

So, for example, say you want to buy a small cap share with a market size of about £3000-worth – that's about what you'd be able to deal in. Market sizes, now called Exchange Market Size, can be found on the London Stock Exchange website (click a quote for the share you are interested in and the EMS appears under 'Trading Information').

One major advantage with IG is that you can deal in AIM (Alternative Investment Market) shares tax-free. You can't put AIM shares in an ISA, so outside of spread betting you may be liable for capital gains tax on bigger wins with these.

The dealer's view

Pete says –

66 We like our clients to educate themselves as much as possible, and indeed new clients get a weekly education email from us for six weeks after they open an account. We want clients to win – as the more they win, the more they will trade with us. 99

I got these emails when I started my account with IG and they're good – they're called 'TradeSense'.

Pete confirms that if you are short of a share and it goes bust you will get paid out full profits from the entire descent to zero! However, you may have to wait for the payout until it is confirmed the company has definitely gone kaput, and it is no longer quoted on the market.

Pete adds –

66 We feel clients are getting more astute with their trades. Day traders do tend to explode, while longer-term traders – or perhaps they should be called investors – tend to be the winners. Those who follow the trend usually come out on top. 99

IG got hit during the start of the recession with a run of customers who couldn't pay them. In fact, its own accounts show something like £16 million was owed by losing clients when things got bad in October 2008. Things have changed since then, and now they will close you out fast if you go over your margin. Pete explains –

66 Traders who go over their limit get an email from us right way to give them time to add funds or to close out positions. If we don't hear from them, we close out trades starting with the oldest. This also protects them as well as us. But we can close trades out rightaway; it's up to the customer to ensure margin is covered. 99

So be warned: do not go over your limit and, if you do, decide how you want to respond *fast*.

After the Visits – My Conclusions

I think any spread bettor who visited either Tradefair or IG Index would – thankfully – be pretty satisfied. Snarling hordes of pinstriped Hitlers entirely failed to materialise. I was happy with what I saw. It seems to me that these two examples of spread firms *do* give you the chance to win, and I hope, if you use some of the rules I outline in this book, you will have a fighting chance to do just that with either of them (or anyone else reputable).

But it's up to you whether you end up a loser or winner with them. It is possible to be a winner, especially if you're not too greedy or too fearful. They **don't** especially want you to lose. And that is the main thing. If you want to take your profits, you can. They are not going to stand in your way. That's the best news of all!

And even better news for me: I'm not visiting any of the others and therefore don't have to get on the Tube for a while!

And now off the record ... anecdotal evidence (AKA amazing how alcohol helps)

So those were my visits to the spread firms. But I have also met those who work for spread betting firms 'out of hours'. In particular, I met a top boss from a spread betting firm at a dinner recently, and even more luckily, he'd had four pints and I'd only had one – so I thought "Here's my chance to find out a few things…"

I was very interested in getting his insider's view on what makes a spread bettor a winner or a loser. I asked –

"So what are the trading patterns of the people who win and what about the people that lose?"

His answer was rather revealing.

He said –

❝ The people that win don't trade as much as the people that lose! ❞

He seemed convinced this was the key to not losing your shirt. Apparently those with more than ten open positions start to lose the plot because they've got too much to watch and start making mistakes. The best usually have six to eight bets on at any one time.

The next secret he let me in on was –

❝ Winners are often those who ask for spreads on firms I've never heard of, rather than the FTSE 100 companies. ❞

Hmm. Interesting! Looks like those who've done their research on some of the smaller companies end up in the money.

And another secret –

❝ Winners often go flat for a few days. ❞

He doesn't mean winners lie down, he means they simply close down all their trades, take profits and losses and simply have a few days without a trade on their account at all.

"It seems to refresh their brains and clear things out," he said. He also explained that sometimes a big winner can turn into an equally big loser –

66 I've seen winning accounts turn into losing accounts because the trader gets overconfident and starts playing with much bigger stakes. We often see people who start winning but then get way too confident and start to put too large stakes on – the winning accounts suddenly turn into losing ones. And the ones that lose the most were those who put all their eggs in one basket and took out one or two big positions. Much better to have a number of balanced positions. 99

What about shorters and buyers, I wondered. Which trades make the money? He said –

66 Most people still go long only – they just can't seem to cope with shorting. People also struggle to be short and long at the same time.

We had some excellent winners during the downturn of 2008 – they shorted the banks like crazy and made a lot – but actually it was a small number compared to those who carried on going long during this time – they lost their shirts. 99

He also revealed that those who hung onto trades tended to lose out. He said –

66 Spread betting is a short-term tool; those holding onto positions for too long often make a loss. In the trade we call these positions that people have held for too long a time, 'short-term trades that went wrong'! 99

Also, those that make the best shorters are apparently those who don't hang onto their shorts for very long. (Oo-er, missus.)

I then asked him if he could allow me access to the accounts of the biggest losers, so I could see what they did and then do the opposite to them, but I guess in the end he just wasn't pissed enough!

7. It's All in the Mind

Yes, it really is. Making or losing money on spread betting is more often based on your brain than what the market does. For example, if you're in a good or bad mood. So I would like to touch on a little psychology.

Psychology (How are you feeling today?)

Who are you and why?

What sort of person lurks inside that brain of yours?

You might feel tempted to skip this section and...oh, have you gone already? All right – well, you paid for this book so you can do what the hell you like, can't you?

Those of you still with me (the sensible ones), you already know that it's your brain plus your emotions that are going to make your spread betting decisions, and you need some understanding of psychology and how it will affect you in this type of trading.

I'm afraid some people just aren't suited to spread betting. It's because they haven't got the right brain for it.

Spread betting is really very simple. Numbers are moving up or down, and you bet on whether the numbers will finish up or down at some point in the future. You have to be on the right side of those numbers. However, get consistently on the wrong side of them, and your money could disappear *fast*: so you need the right sort of temperament.

What you need to do is take an honest look at yourself and decide how you'd handle it if you started losing, or things got out of control.

Take a deep breath...

Did you know your spread betting will actually cause you to release hormones – and that applies to the men as well as the women reading this? If you start losing money, according to the experts, you release a stress hormone called cortisol. (Hey, I'm not making this up – Google it if you don't believe me.) This hormone can lead to you feeling helpless and panicked.

The question is: can you handle stress?

Or are you going to run around like Corporal Jones in *Dad's Army* when things don't go your way?

Do you think you'll be able to stay calm and unemotional? Because that's what you need to do.

John Coates from Cambridge University, who used to run a trading desk, told the *Telegraph*:

> " If elevated cortisol exposure lingers and becomes chronic, it begins to hinder the wits. Cortisol is especially stimulated by conditions of novelty, uncertainty and uncontrollability – conditions that describe a trader's life during a crisis.

If the uncertainty that comes with high volatility persists for a long time, then cortisol can have pervasive effects on the way we think. In particular, excessive cortisol causes us to recall mostly negative memories and to find risk where none may exist. Furthermore, it may impair the functioning of the brain in ways that make us less analytical and more emotionally reactive. **"**

So you need to be the type of character who can deal with this hormone and the feelings it brings. If you have a losing streak, the feelings of negativity you experience can overwhelm you, make you bet like crazy and lose even more.

(Nothing more than) feelings

If you're going to be a good spread bettor you have to understand how you feel and learn to cut it off from your trading decisions. Spread betting should be looked upon as a business. Don't get personal with it or you will do your brain (and your account balance) in.

Here's an interesting mail that I received:

" Unfortunately I opened an account with a spread-bet firm today and have lost £500 on my first bet. I went long on Aviva early this morning and stupidly put the stop loss back and back hoping it would recover. It didn't and I feel sick. I'm very new to this trading lark and I'm female (dumb and blonde) – I cannot afford to lose anymore or to feel as I do at the moment so I have come on your site to be cheered up. Thanks Robbie (must go as hubby is coming in the front door and don't want him to know how much I lost). I'll be opening another account and coming back to fix it all tomorrow. **"**

Several interesting points about psychology come from this short mail.

It's easy to see this would-be trader is in the wrong mindset right from the word go. She made a fatal mistake with her very first trade. She had no intention of losing £500 but she "put the stop loss back and back hoping it would recover".

What happened there?

She became emotionally involved with this share from the off, instead of letting the stop take her out unemotionally.

And now things have got worse: now she's got a desire for revenge. She's going to open another spread bet account. And the worst of all?

She's already made a screw up and she's going to hide it from her husband. Hiding things like this means she's on the road to a gambling problem. What she ought to do is share what happened with her husband – admit the mistake. She'd feel better. Because if you find yourself hiding losses from your partner, then something is going seriously wrong psychologically.

It really is best to share losses with a close one, not hide them. Otherwise, you know what'll happen? You'll be in a bad mood when trades go wrong, and you'll take it out on those close to you. You could end up having rows over something else, when all you're doing is having a go because you're cross with yourself. You can see this on bulletin boards where people fight with each other when actually they are really angry with themselves.

Talking of moods, trading in a bad mood is NOT a good idea, as this reader shows:

❝ My first SB [spread bet] was a small FTSE one, which went to a nice profit (10% of the account size) so I closed the position. But after that everything went badly. I tried to catch up the FTSE but I made a typo and opened a £14.70 per point on the FTSE (instead of £1.47). As soon as it was validated, my stop loss got triggered as the FTSE dropped over 25pts in a matter of seconds – and that wrote off all my gains and a large chunk of my SB account. The stop loss was way too close for trading the FTSE, it was bound to happen. A few minutes later and I would have been in profit, but it was closed and I was there with a large chunk of my SB account gone.

I also had open an FPM [Faroe Petrol] SB that saved my day and recovered my loss as it was a share that I know quite well. Then I re-opened another FTSE bet, which was not too large, not too small. Gave me one day of profit. Next day, while shopping, I checked my account with my spread firm's mobile trader interface. They have the sell button on a key, which is used as 'back' on many of my applications, and as a reflex I hit the sell key and closed the FPM position in profit. I realised it as it was happening, but could not stop it.

I was so angry at myself that I re-opened the position straightaway but I lost a few points in the deal. And when I re-opened the FPM position, I had to put a way higher stop loss than set up originally, as the deposit on my account was not large enough anymore. Obviously what was bound to happen, did happen: the share dropped. My stop loss did not trigger when it should have, but I manually closed half of the position to stop the exposure. This was a bad move again, as by Friday close I would have been in profit again!

Anyway, it is all down to emotions and stupid mistakes by ME :) I remember reading that one should not trade when not in a good mood (thinking too much about personal stuff, etc) and I can confirm that it is the case for me! 〞

This is the kind of mindset you can get into – all mixed emotions and chasing silly trades that aren't properly planned. And here's another one whose mind has been churned over by spread betting:

❝ I think of myself as really streetwise, ahead of the game – till I started doing this. The more I'm in it, the less I feel I know. I need to be able to learn when to enter and exit. At best I just follow trends and miss it by a long shot. I must be just addicted to stress – f**k me I'd better get this right or I will be outside Brixton tube selling the *Big Issue*... 〞

This spread bettor is completely caught up with emotion and his mindset is all wrong. He really needs to come out of all bets and stand aside. If you start to feel like this, calmly re-evaluate what you are doing.

However, this email I received is even worse:

❝ I started spread betting about a year and a half ago and I have been hammered, to say the least. Spread betting really canes you. I was doing really well at the start and then started to get hammered and tried to double up to get my money back – you know the rest of the story here. I finally counted it up tonight. I'd been thinking I'd lost about £100,000-£150,000...mate, try £315,000. Anyway, I've got a few good books and I'm going back to basics again. There is only one consolation; I have the ability to make big money very quickly...or lose big money very quickly as well, as you can see. 〞

I guess that mail really speaks for itself; the guy is an addict. He should stop – yesterday. But today would be a bloody good start! Which leads me on to...

Ordinary share dealing vs. spread betting

Cost-wise there isn't much in it between the two – what you win in not paying stamp duty and commission with spread betting is usually balanced out by the extra spread on both ends of the trade. But psychologically, as also discussed elsewhere in the book, there is and you have to get to grips with that.

As one of my readers describes:

> " I find spread betting psychologically harder than normal share trading. One effect of this has been that I make my stop losses far too tight – being too prudent. And I'm still doing it.
>
> I bought CHTR at 702.4 only for my stop loss of 677.4 to be hit an hour later – a ridiculously tight SL of 3.6% that I would never have imposed on an ordinary purchase of actual shares.
>
> There is a strong temptation to convert a stop loss into a limit order that yields a stupidly small profit once it is possible. The pressure to do this increases directly with the losses you have recently made.
>
> Price spikes can be dramatic in spread betting. I placed an order to buy which I saw activated immediately as it jumped into my open orders list, only to find the position had disappeared when I looked back up at the screen a few moments later. A vicious down spike had hit the purchase *and* the not unreasonable stop loss almost simultaneously! Very depressing.
>
> If you put a bet on the FTSE without a stop loss, don't go and have breakfast; you can spend an agonising morning, finger hovering over the buy or sell button, if you got the direction wrong. Been there.
>
> Spread betting results after 12 months' share dealing: huge losses. Ordinary share dealing; showing a 25% rise on current portfolio with other good profits already banked.
>
> For me, the explanation is psychological, but I'm getting better. "

An interesting mail. This reader was fine with his normal account but screwed up with a spread betting one. And it was all to do with psychology, as he admits. He got clobbered by shares moving violently. In a normal account he may have held on but in a spread betting one he panicked or his stops got hit.

You might think what I've said about psychology is cobblers and that all these mistakes and situations will never happen to you. You're perfectly capable of taking care of yourself and all that. But please be careful and consider not betting for a while if you feel emotional, things get out of control, or even if bad things are happening in your personal life.

Key things to watch out for are:

- heavy emotional feelings regarding your trades,
- arguments with close ones,
- feelings of helplessness.

Keep your feelings out of your spread betting and treat it as a business.

Fear and Greed

Whilst the danger of fear and greed is an old stock market byword, it's also particularly true in the world of spread betting. In fact, they're more dangerous here – you can get wiped out quicker. If you let either of these two get hold of you, there's only one thing that'll happen: you lose!

Greed

Greed is almost certainly the biggest danger for spread bettors. What tends to happen is that the spread bettor is doing well, the money is flooding into the accounts and the bettor then gets way too greedy. It's his undoing. The same characteristic of spread betting which gain him swift success, gain him equally swift failure: the leverage makes for quick and often unbearable losses when too much is staked and stops aren't set.

Greed – example 1

This from the *Mail on Sunday* in late 2009 [edited for length]:

66 The City financier who apparently went missing while owing clients millions of pounds finally emerged from hiding yesterday – and blamed the losses on his gambling addiction. Nick Levene, 45, nicknamed Beano because of his extravagant lifestyle, faces a criminal inquiry after investing huge sums for tycoons, but failing to deliver their promised riches.

Tracked down by *The Mail on Sunday*, he revealed he has been receiving ongoing 'treatment for gambling addiction' at a Priory clinic. He admitted: 'I have lost millions of pounds because of my addiction to spread betting – it is in the region of £50 million to £70 million.'

He took increasingly risky positions in an attempt to recover but it brought only further disaster. From his office in Mayfair, he could only watch as the numbers flickering on the screen on his desk told a painful story: his clients' investment funds were being wiped out, million after million, and there was nothing he could do. 'It was horrific – like watching a plane going down,' he says.

His worried investors, some of the richest tycoons in the land, would then ring him and were reassured that all was fine: Levene, though feeling sick to his stomach, told them he was making them millions. 'I had become dishonest and deceitful,' he says. 'Living like this was dreadful. I couldn't think, sleep or eat. I was in a bubble.'

In his first bet on stock market futures he lost £25,000, which although leaving him 'shocked', was not enough to put him off. 'I went back to have one more go, then one more and so on.' He recalls winning £50,000 'and then it went to winning and losing hundreds of thousands and then millions'. After winning his first £1 million spread bet on the futures market, he was taken to dinner by Jonathan Hufford, managing director of Spreadex.

Levene says: 'I wanted to prove myself. Last week, I got a letter from my father saying that my downfall could be down to greed. I don't think I was greedy. I was over-ambitious and liked making a quick buck.' **"**

What a story! But one to learn from – and if you feel you have any of the gambling or addictive traits shown by Nick be especially careful.

Greed – example 2

Mike Ashley, billionaire owner of Newcastle Football Club, lost £129 million gambling on spread bets by the end of 2008, according to the *Telegraph*. The papers reported that he gambled £300,000 a point on HBOS to go up at £8.80. His exposure, even for a rich man, was rather a lot – £24 million! The *Mirror* reckoned it was more than that and said Ashley had lost £300 million on his HBOS bet.

Well, take your pick on the amounts – whatever, they were large, even to him. The temptation again was to simply put way too much on one share or one bet. He thought along the lines of: this share's gone down a lot – it's got to go back up!

No no no. No.

If it were that simple, everyone else would be doing it too, and we'd all be instant millionaires. It is *never* that simple.

Of course, where he went *terribly* wrong was in not setting a stop loss and allowing the loss to build up to silly levels. At 880, a stop should have been in at around the 800 mark – something that would have saved him multi-millions. But it seems greed took over, turned him, and quickly relieved him of the GDP of the Isle of Wight.

Greed kills. It is to trading what drinking is to driving. You think you're invincible. In fact, you're simply heading for a tree.

If you haven't got this yet, read the story a dealer tells in the chapter where I visit spread-bet firms, about a guy who started with £10k, got it to £500k, then lost it again. Again, he got greedy, used too much leverage and wanted to make money way too fast.

Successful spread betting is about consistency, not casinos.

Fear

This is the other main emotion with spread betting and it strikes in three ways:

1. Fear of **taking a loss quickly** – by that I mean fear of crystallising a loss, and, in the end, a dent to the ego.

2. Fear of **losing a small profit**, and taking it too early when it would have been better to let it run.

3. Fear leading to a **general panic**, where suddenly all decisions are made emotionally and, because of that, are often the wrong ones.

Of the two emotions fear is probably the less dangerous of the two. At least fear might cause you to get out of something! But probably the worst thing about fear is it will make you trade too much. Your feelings of fear will cause you to sell a loser quickly but then buy back in the moment it starts going up, as the fear subsides. But then the fear starts up again the moment it falls. Stay fearful and you will forever be trading but never making.

Fear and greed have to be overcome to be a good spread bettor. The best way to overcome both emotions is to set a stop loss, which is discussed elsewhere in the book. Then the exit decision is already made before your emotions set in.

It's a War Out There

I hate to be the bearer of bad news, but don't think for a second that the market is a nice place to spread bet. There are NO nice people out there, okay? The moment you push your first button on your spread betting account, you are into battle.

You need your shields up (that was for *Star Trek* fans – you know you love it, resistance is futile), and your lightsaber ready for action (see, I like *Star Wars* fans too). It's you against other people – you are a seller of something and someone else will be a buyer; or you are a buyer and someone else will be opposing you. And you need to be on the right side more often than the wrong one.

Who are your opponents?

Anyone and everyone. You'll be up against short-term traders just wanting to grab a couple of points. You may be up against a market maker. Market makers are clever and devious. You've got to be good! And, indeed, you may not even be up against a human being at all! It may be an unemotional robot taking the opposite end of your trade. But who or whatever it is, if you win, someone else loses.

And to win, you have got to be focused and disciplined.

THERE GOES DARTH TRADER – OFF TO DO BATTLE ON THE SPREAD BETTING FRONTLINE

www.petedredge.co.uk

8. The Top 11 Mistakes Made By New Spread Bettors

I've already covered some of the following at greater length in the book but I thought a summary, along with a few extra points, would be useful. I was going to make it a top 10 but it came out at 11. Have the extra one on me!

1. Allowing positions to run away into huge losses

If you don't set a stop loss, you're asking for trouble. The temptation is to hang on to the losers and allow them to carry on, losing even more money in the hope that they will come back. It's nearly always much better to quickly cut a position that's losing a small amount. You can always get back into it, even a bit lower down. The absolute worst thing you can do is let the big losses build up.

Always take smaller losses quickly!

2. Setting too tight stop losses

So, yes, set a stop loss, but be careful on the stop level. If you're trading a volatile stock, setting a too tight stop all the time can be a disastrous move. It's understandable, you want to be out of something fast with a small loss by setting a tight stop. But the problem with doing this on volatile shares is that you are pretty much asking for each of your trades to be closed out too early. Think carefully about where to place your stop. Many traders get closed out as the market opens with wide spreads – don't be one of them and set sensible stops a reasonable distance away. Use levels below resistance and support to make sure those stops do not get hit inappropriately.

3. Trading forex

Nearly everyone loses at trading forex, so I have been told. In fact you are not doing badly if you break even. So my view is: don't touch it. You could easily end up like this chap who wrote to me –

> ❝ I've been trading Forex, primarily GBP/USD, for the past of 6 months and I keep losing. I do find Forex to be very 'trendy', in that when it's going one way it seems to follow it until it hits some support or resistance and then retraces. It usually bounces off every 50-cent mark too.
>
> However, that said, I can never seem to make a consistent profit. Very often I get stopped out only for the tide to suddenly turn and go my way again. Grrrr. Believe me when I say that on more than one occasion the £ has risen to my exact stop and then fallen back. And I don't pick obvious stops either! Of course, being stopped out is only to be expected when Cable [Dollar/Pound – Ed] moves 200 points a day and I have only £100 in my account (£1 per point). So do you think I should not bother on the Forex front? I don't want to move my stop away another 50 points, because, quite frankly, I don't want to lose £100 a trade if it goes against me. ❞

Hey, you can guess my answer. It is perhaps possible for a very seasoned trader to make money out of this, but the trader would probably concentrate on this and nothing else *and* have iron self-will. The thing is: why bother trying to make money here when there are easier ways, and you know for a fact that nearly everyone loses?

4. Over-leveraging

There's a story in this book of someone who generated huge wins of over a quarter of a million, but ended up owing the spread firm after he over-leveraged. Over-leveraging is the same as using the whole of your credit card limit when you can't afford it. Trouble is, unlike credit-card companies the spread firm can want all its money back immediately. You can't send them a minimum monthly payment. By over-leveraging I mean, for example, having £20k worth of exposure when you only have £3k in the bank to cover your losses. It's madness. Stick to the money you actually have and don't leverage up.

5. System addict

A punter will buy a supa dupa 'system'. This system claims amazing success rates. The ad blurb will assure you that all you've gotta do is follow the system and you'll be RICH! (or even RICH!!!!!!) And it's all so EASY!

Believe me, the only person making money will be the clever sod that sold you the system. Because if the supa dupa system worked, the person trying to sell it to you would be in Barbados surrounded by a bevy of beauties. He certainly wouldn't be sitting in an office in Slough trying to flog you a system.

6. Overtrading

This is the greatest danger of spread betting losers – getting addicted. You love all the flashing lights. While your partner is busy watching *EastEnders* you're busy getting burned trading the Dow up and down, down and up – bashing buttons feverishly to get back the money you lost.

It's a fact that the biggest losers are those who trade too much. If you've been placing ten or more trades a day, you are probably in this camp. Stop and rethink. If you can't stop, you may have a gambling problem and need to seek help. (www.gambleaware.co.uk).

7. Playing indices too much

Instead of trading shares, you suddenly got addicted to playing the FTSE 100 – maybe even making loads of trades on it in one day, taking quick profits here and quick losses there. At 4.30pm you come away from your computer absolutely shattered. You didn't do the work you were supposed to do that day. In fact, your normal work is suffering – yet you might only be making a tiny profit, or more likely losses. You're wasting your energy over a few points here and there.

Better to waste your energy down the pub with a few pints here and there instead. At least you could relax.

The sheer pace and frequency of index movements could see you become grumpy and bad-tempered and caring about nothing but those numbers going up or down. If you recognise yourself here, have a good think.

Overplaying indices = losses. I promise.

8. Getting emotional and losing it

F*$*!@ b!*@§*, a£*! and even c@!*=!.

We discussed emotions earlier, but if you do find yourself shouting at the screen and blaming everyone else for your losses then you may be losing it.

You MUST keep a grip on your emotions when spread betting; stay calm and under control. If you are spread betting you must consider it a business, not a hobby. And in business there is no time for emotion. Look at your trades calmly and don't fall in love with a company – they are just items to be traded. If the trade isn't working out then dump it, don't get emotional. Keep a clear head.

And don't have too many pints at lunchtime and then trade either!

9. Buying against the trend or trying to spot a turn

This can end in disaster. You think, "This company's share price has gone up quite a bit. It must be time for it to go down. I'll go short." But it keeps going up, you keep your short open and you end up a sore loser. This can happen time and time again. Better to let the trend of your share dictate what you do than trying to guess when the trend has changed.

Try to follow trends and not go against them, being a smartarse.

Remember: your few quid will be flattened by the rush of much bigger money. Trends stay in place longer than you think and they often go against all rational logic.

 Never forget: markets can be irrational far longer than you can stay solvent.

10. Greed

"Greed is the biggest barrier to winning at spread betting," one trader told me.

He thinks it's similar to betting on the horses. A punter has a couple of big wins and then gets greedy. He ups his stake, maybe chucks all he has on an odds-on punt that comes second, and walks out of the betting shop with nothing – rather than taking his earlier wins and pocketing them.

The best advice from this trader was, "If you win, bank some of it." He doesn't mean put it in your spread betting account, he quite literally means BANK it. Yes, put it in the bank. Keep it safe from your own tempted hands!

I think the problem is that, after a few wins, punters look at their accounts and think, "Oooooh, now I can bet even more and with even bigger amounts!" Oh greedy one, you will be undone.

And finally, but most importantly...

11. Not cutting losers and running profits

I know, I can say this till I'm blue in the face and you still won't do it will you?

If you don't cut your losses quickly you will, eventually, lose overall. It really is that simple.

Sometimes it's even worth cutting them before it hits your stop if you think you got it wrong. You can always get back in. Remember: you can still win overall by taking lots of small losses.

Meanwhile, don't take quick profits of a couple of quid just because you had a run of losers and you're desperate to bank a winner. Have the confidence to hold the winners for a while – it's amazing when you do have a winner how much more it can carry on going up. Remember: you can always just raise your stop if you're not sure about it – and think about using trailing stops to protect the profit if you are unsure.

So while cutting losses and running profits might be a cliché, it really really works!

PART II:

DOING IT

9. Strategies I Use

In this section I explain some of the strategies I use. Some may be obvious, some you might find strange. All I can tell you is they seem to work for me!

And then, after this, we'll take a look at how I put these strategies into action, with a study of some of my trades.

News-driven events

Sometimes news breaks about a particular event, and this pushes the market in a share or index one way or the other. Often I find the market greatly overreacts to such news, so there is short-term money to be made in determining if the market will go back to where it was before the event happened. This can often be quite straightforward.

An example: late in 2009, Dubai said it couldn't handle some of its debts and this caused the FTSE to tumble 172 points. My immediate thought was: this will blow over really quickly. It's not that much of a big deal. So, early the morning after, I went long on the FTSE – I didn't think such a big fall was warranted. And this paid off big-time for me, with a profit of over £1000 in less than two days.

Another example was swine flu. In the early days there was some panic that we'd end up in a sci-fi horror movie scenario: *28 Days Later* but with more bacon (presumably – I'm no medical expert). But again it looked like one of those things people like to over-hype – and the market duly overreacted. Airline shares were especially hit. So, after a week of worry, I bought British Airways, which I was sure had been oversold; and again this proved a decent strategy and another good profit banked.

Sometimes bad news can hit a share – and if you wait a bit you can grab a bounce, especially after a few days of falls when in essence it is a short-term news event that isn't as bad as people think. This even applies when, in the long term, the news event does turn out to be bad: people are often willing to be persuaded otherwise in the meantime, as you never can know just how bad things ultimately will get. An example is BP, which sprung the now famous leak in April 2010, causing the share price to fall 40% over a couple of weeks. I waited till the price hit 350p, then saw a company announcement saying its price fall was unwarranted. That prompted me to spread bet the shares, buying them up and giving me a quick reward of 50 points, a £1000 profit over a week, as the market accepted their reassurance.

Another example is if an accounting 'irregularity' is reported. Said share of course falls dramatically, but the key is to check the company's statement to see if they think the irregularity will actually affect profits.

Dragon Oil announced such a problem and its shares slumped. But I noted how they'd added that it would not affect profits and they pretty much said it didn't affect the bottom line. So I bought the shares and they ended up trebling.

Buying after a news statement disappoints can be a good strategy too. The news causes punters to bale out and often a price just sinks far too much. For example, if profits are down 10% and the shares get marked down 30% on panic selling, then it could be a good time for a quick buy. Watch for tons of distressed sellers getting out at once, wait for the share to stabilise and then POUNCE before everyone piles in. Once they have, sell it, and take profits!

I now have a spread betting account just for this kind of trade – I call it my 'news' account. It gives me tons of firepower to go in when something happens.

Buy on fear...

Buying on fear can really pay dividends. A few years ago the market would tumble on some catastophe and the fall would last for some time. But these days the market reacts to these events very quickly by marking everything down and then it tends to come back up quickly.

In March 2009, people really thought all the banks were going to crash. The fears were overdone and the markets had slumped way too much. Anyone buying spread bets around this time would have been quids in a few weeks later. I can remember buying Barclays on the spreads at around 80p and they quickly trebled in value.

...sell on greed

Everything looking rosy? Shares well up? Papers talking about economic recovery, lots of new books with titles like *The Next Big Thing*? Cabbie telling you which shares to buy?

That's a great time to bank some spread-bet profits, or indeed go short!

Just as fear takes the market too low, greed takes it too high. And often the best time to get out is when everyone is happy. Sad, but true. In effect, markets usually take things to extremes and rise too high or fall too far.

Short on debt

My other book, *The Naked Trader*, covers debt and how to expose a company's debt in more depth, and it can be a great strategy. If a company has a large debt then you have a great reason to lob in a short because if it's really big then at some point it will have to make a cash call to investors, probably with a rights issue – and a rights issue almost always drags a share price down. See big debt: think short.

Specialise

I like getting to know a small number of shares very well. I know about their profits, their losses, their charts, where they have been and who they've been hanging about with. If you can do this with five or six shares then after a while I find you can get a feel for their movements.

I know about 20 shares very well – so well that I can quickly spot any odd movements or anything unusual happening.

As mentioned earlier in the book, one of my favourites is Wolseley, which between 2008 and 2009 moved in a tight trading range of around 200 points (1300 to 1500) allowing plenty of shorter-term gains.

Getting to know everything about a small number of shares, how and why and when they move, can really benefit your trading. So get specialising! This may be made easier if through your area of work you know a certain company or sector well.

Make best friends with a few shares, know all about them and make money – when they go down as well as up.

Use charts

I'm not an advocate of using charts on their own *per se*, but they can be of immense help – especially when a share keeps repeating the same pattern. For example, as you can see from Wolseley's chart, it just kept on hitting 1500 then falling back a number of times, which made a short near 1500 easy to put on, followed by a long at the 1300 area. Or at 1400. It didn't much matter. It was so easy to short anytime it got near 1500, because it just could not get through that barrier.

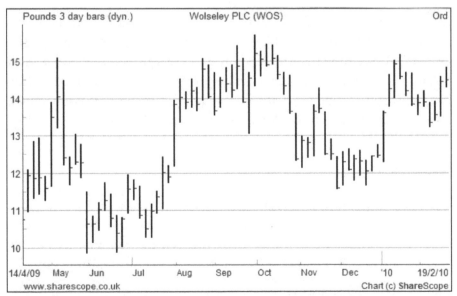

Wolseley, resistance at 1500, support around 1300/1400

Keeping tabs on the history of a share or index is a useful piece of knowledge, especially as history often repeats itself.

Short newspaper tips

This might sound a bit perverse, but if you're looking for a really short-term short it can pay to short tips on smaller companies made in the bigger papers or even the investment magazines.

Why?

Because market makers know that people will buy in because they read about it in the paper. And what do they do? Mark the price up at the start of the day. People read the tip, unwittingly buy at the often much higher price, and the market makers then lower the price, forcing out those that bought and making themselves an instant profit. This can be a really good strategy if you disagree with the tip.

My best result was when a company called Spice was tipped by a national paper. The price went much higher the following day, but I saw that the company's debt was enormous and happily shorted into the strength. A few weeks later the shares slumped, making the short well into profit.

Go with the trend

Don't try to second-guess a turning point. An amazing number of spread-bet traders think that because an index or a share price has gone up or gone down a lot it must be time to go against the trend. And they keep going long or short and lose money all the while as they get stopped out – because the trend just continues.

For example, say the FTSE has gone up 300 points. Hah, time to short it!

But why?

You might be right and the FTSE might be too high because, say, the economy is still in bad shape. That won't, however, necessarily stop it going up further. It's a bit like you trying to walk backwards through a stampede. You will get flattened by the millions of bulls.

Try to go with a trend that is still intact – trying to guess a top or a bottom is a bad idea. It's much better to ride the trend up or down once it is obvious that it has already changed.

News!

" *Buy the rumour, sell the news.* "

This is is something of a cliché in stock-market circles, but it's a cliché that is often accurate.

Traders often buy a share in anticipation of good news, and when the good news materialises they sell the share (there's no point in hanging on, they've made their money, time to move on to the next share). And as the traders sell, they will usually be selling to novice investors who do not realise that they are at the end of the food chain and the last to hear the news – they end up enthusiastically buying the share without realising that the news is already in the price and that there are no more buyers after them to come into the market to help drive the shares up further. The traders' action of selling after the news announcement will often be referred to as profit-taking, and the share takes a hit.

In fact, holding a spread betting position in a share over the period of a news announcment by the company can be a dangerous activity, and many traders avoid doing so. Main market companies have to produce four news updates per year – half-year results, full year results and two interim updates – and it is therefore fairly easy to avoid holding a trade on those dates.

Say, for example, you trade a share regularly. It goes up and down and you're happy making money out of it using a trading range. But make sure you don't hold a position on statement day; get back in when a new trading range establishes itself.

Find out when a company's report or statement is due. They are usually around the same date each year. Companies usually put out their forthcoming statement dates and plenty of sites and magazines list them too.

Another way of playing it is to wait for a couple of days after the results and *then* buy. If the news was good, then let the profit-takers jump in and sell up. Once you can see the share has established a new base and buyers are coming in, that could be time to buy.

Short a profits warning

One thing you must remember: spread betting gives you the chance to short, so do look out for opportunities, especially profit warnings. It's amazing how one warning can often lead to a couple of others – so if you see a company which has put out something negative, keep an eye on the price. You're looking for a warning that might affect the share for a while rather than perhaps a one-off news event.

New issues

Sometimes new shares come onto the market – see *The Naked Trader* for a whole chapter on these. It can be worth spread betting these as well as buying them as normal shares, if you like the look of the company. Quite often new entrants do very well in their first few weeks of trading, so why not consider spread betting one?

The thing to watch for is that the share in question might not be available to deal online on its first day of trading, as the spread-bet firms may not have set them up yet. But it should only take a phone call to get a quote.

Also, and even better, sometimes a spread-bet firm will quote a new issue *before* it has been listed, in a kind of grey market in its shares. So you can sometimes get in a week *before* flotation! I've done this a couple of times. Anyway, it's something worth thinking about.

I've spread bet many new issues over the years and often with great success, including Hunting, Wellstream, New Brit and Petrofac. Usually it initially took a phone call but online dealing was set up pretty quickly. Other more recent issues that have done well include SuperGroup and Essar.

Use Level II

I was thinking about covering Level II and the order book because I do use it a lot to help me with short-term timing. The trouble is, whenever I try to explain it in writing it's just impossible! Which is why you won't find any good books on it. The only way I find I can teach it is live at my seminars, using live markets. It's the only way.

Level II shows you what is behind a share price – where the market makers are positioned, and, in bigger shares, at what prices people want to buy and sell. I use it all the time and wish I could explain it in a book. It is just too hard – the one thing I suggest is to concentrate using it on your favourite stocks and get to learn how it works slowly. I often use it to decide if I should really press the sell or buy button or whether I can wait a bit.

If you trade an awful lot with one spread firm you may be offered it for free, otherwise ADVFN offer it via me for £299. Mail me if you are interested or you'd like to come to a seminar where I show how it works live. You'll then understand how impossible it is to explain it on paper.

One thing, though: it is almost useless to try and use it on FTSE 100 shares, so if you only trade those I wouldn't bother. Its best use is for FTSE 250 shares and below.

How do I find shares to trade?

As I said at the start, I assume you have done some share trading or investing in the past and already have some ideas of where to find shares (this is covered in great detail in *The Naked Trader*). So I'm not going to dwell on this, except to explain that I get quite a few ideas for my spread bets from ADVFN's premium Top Lists.

You need its Bronze membership to get these – which I think is worth every penny.

The premium Top Lists, especially the breakouts list, really help me to find spread bets. I use the 12-week or 52-week break-up lists to find longs, and the 12- and 52-week breakdowns to find shorts. In effect this is technical analysis done for you (i.e. finding shares where something interesting is happening either to the upside or downside).

In addition, you can find ideas on stocks in the news and by watching the company reports when they are released every morning. Mail me if you want this.

Conclusion

Of course there are so many possible strategies. You will hopefully find one or a few that suit you over time. We all have different personalities, different times that we can trade, and other factors, and therefore some strategies that suit me won't suit you. I hope one or two of my strategies give you something useful to think about and provide a basis for you to develop your own strategies.

10. Trading Examples

I thought it would help to have a chapter that looked at some real trades I put on. I'll go through why I put on each trade and what happened to it.

First, a look at my shorts. [Ladies may like to look away at this point. – Ed]

Short trades

Shorting is just jargon for trying to make money from a share or an index as it goes down. You lose if it goes up.

It hit the headlines during the downturn of 2008-9 because the practice was blamed for markets supposedly falling further than they should. Which to me is mostly bunkum. Very few people actually short anyway. The authorities even banned shorts of banks for a while. It made no difference, as bank share prices continued to fall anyway!

Many people, especially new traders, find the idea of shorting a bit strange. I've spoken to many people at seminars and they tell me they "just can't handle the idea" of shorting. I'm not sure why this is. I guess we have all been programmed over the years to follow orthodox investment lines: buying shares that you want to invest in, as opposed to selling shares that you don't even own! But shorting is one of the main benefits of spread betting. Therefore you ought to seriously consider shorting as part of your trading armoury.

However, you need to work out *why* you are shorting something. Here are some of my ideas.

A Short Note: Before I proceed, one thing to emphasise is – if you get one of your shorts wrong – get out quick! I set very tight stops on shorts because if the market starts to rise, however rubbish you think a certain company is, it will probably rise along with the market as a whole.

What am I looking for in a short?

- A company in some sort of trouble, preferably with big debt compared to its profits

- a share in some kind of longer-term downtrend, though it's possible to work with a short-term uptrend that's stalling

- a share in a sector that's out of favour

- if another company in the same area or sector has reported a drop in sales or a profits warning,

- a share chart where a price keeps bumping up against the same level only to keep retreating.

Just before I start, a reminder (not because I necessarily think you're thick, mind; just to, you know, drill it home): to short a share (or bet on it to go down) remember to press 'sell' or the down arrow! When taking a profit or a loss press the 'buy' or 'close trade' button!

www.petedredge.co.uk

Real short examples

Without further ado here are some examples.

Corin

- Reason: Poor sales and profit warnings.

- Spread bet: Short at 80p. Target 60p. Stop 85p.

Corin had some funky hip-replacement technology, which all sounded fine, but it just kept issuing profit warnings – it appeared not enough people wanted to buy into it. Cue a short from me after another very cautious statement. Added to that it appeared there was some debt building up too. And it wasn't making any money.

Profit warnings, like buses, tend to come in threes. So if you short after the first one or two and the shares keep falling you can usually make some money.

Corin

I did £40 a point. You can see from the chart it went up to 85ish but started sinking badly after releasing results, which was when I got in. You can see how I got my target price of 60 as it's where the share always seemed to bottom out in the past.

I came out of the trade at 61 to make £760 profit:

```
£40 x (80p - 61p) = £760
```

I closed because the price of Corin was constantly supported at roughly 60p. Or in other words the market didn't appear to think it was worth any less than 60 at the time. So, nice trade!

I hope Ed isn't lazy and checks all my maths on these, 'cos I know if any are wrong I'll get the same email day after day pointing out the mistake till I go bananas and ask for all copies of this book to be pulped! [Don't worry, I've got the calculator out. – Ed]

Spice

- Reason: High debt/newspaper tip caused price spike

- Spread bet: Short at 94. Target 70. Stop 105.

This was simply a debt short for me. Nothing much wrong with this company. It made decent sums but I felt it had overextended with debt of more than £110m on profits of £23m. And with a false rise because of a newspaper tip I did £50 a point at 94 and came out at 55 for a profit of £1950 (39 x 50).

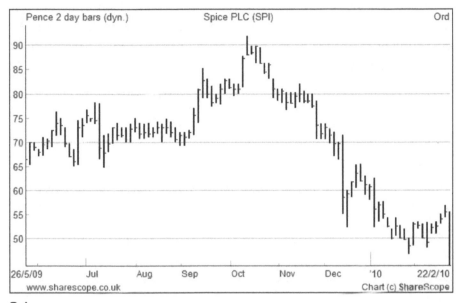

Spice

You can see from the chart my target was 70 because the share kept bouncing off that level in the past (support). However, I kept hold of the bet because it went straight through support and could only find new support again at 50. At that point buyers kept wading in and that looked a good point to bank.

As it turned out, the share went even lower to 40p. Still, a good profit so no complaints. It eventually went to 30 at which point it began to look a bargain and I bought it – and am still holding it while writing this!

Imagination

- Reason: Valuation looked too high.

- Spread bet: Short at 254. Target 220. Stop 270.

Of course not every short is going to work out and, like everyone else, of course I will have losers. However, I get out pretty darn fast and take a loss if I realise I've made a mistake. Which is exactly what I did here.

The value of Imagination had grown to a whopping £600m or so, yet it was only making about £8m. The market valuation looked very large – but it was large because Imagination makes chips (no, not the ketchup-dunking kind!) and the market imagined (geddit?) that the company would strike it big with a large deal or two. I decided there was too much hope there.

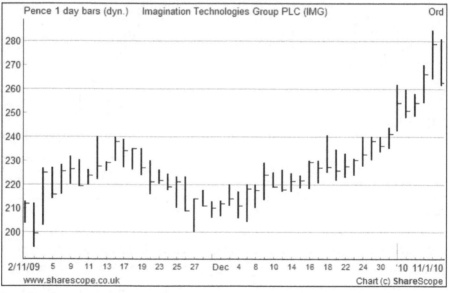

Imagination

But take a look at the chart. It rose like nobody's business. *Where was I going wrong?*

I was trying to go against a very strong uptrend and so I paid the price. Remember the market can be 'wrong' about your share for longer than you can stay solvent!

The short never looked like working out and the share price breezily kept going up, rudely ignoring my educated position! In fact it was rising strongly so I quickly closed out at 262, taking a loss of £160. And just as well as it kept on going up. Believe me, it's much better to take a quick loss on shorts than hang on and hope (and lose even more money).

Hands up guv, I got it wrong, but no big damage done, move right along now, nothing to see here … (I bet it'll be a short again soon!)

Wolseley

The repeat short winner!

- Reason: Big debt and big resistance.

- Spread bet: Short at 1492. Target 1220. Stop 1550.

I actually shorted Wolseley quite a lot; all reasonably short-term shorts making me nice sums. First of all the company had big debt. Secondly, its sector was struggling. But best of all it doesn't take a genius to look at the chart (ahem, look at the chart then ... pay attention those at the back!) and see that whenever it gets up to near the 1500 level it falls back. So there is huge resistance for the price going any higher. Support on the chart, as you can see, is at 1000 and 1200.

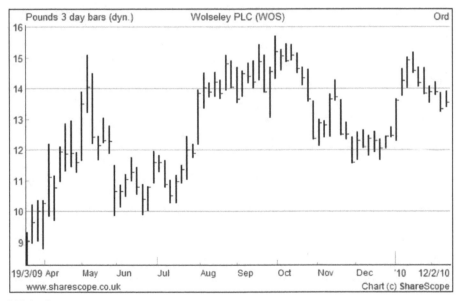

Wolseley

In fact, look closely and you could have shorted this any number of times from 1450-ish to a little above 1550 downwards with very little risk. Simply placing a stop loss at 1550 would be enough to keep you in the trade.

So I shorted Wolseley for £5 at 1492. Oh, and remember exposure? A £5 bet at this price is the same as 500 shares, so:

```
500 x 1492 = £7460 exposure
```

I came out at 1230 when buyers began to come in, for a profit of £1310 (262 x 5).

As I said, I repeated this kind of trading a number of times.

Of course, a trading pattern will not last forever and something usually happens to change it – my guess is it will change to another tradable pattern.

Man Group

- Reason: Profits warning and broke down through support.

- Spread bet: Short at 292. Target 250. Stop 310.

Oh man! What a lovely short, though I did take profits too early. I shorted for £20 a point. A double whammy here – this hedge fund issued a warning after its (nice laugh here) trading system proved a crock and made loads of duff trades! And you can see from the chart it fell through 300 after it had been supported there previously. A lovely short indeed – with a target of 250, where it had found previous support.

Man Group

However, it kept going through 250 and I closed at 240 for a profit of £1040. Actually my exit was wrong – this carried on falling and I should have held on. Never mind. Still a good trade.

Yell

- Reason: Huge debt, dated business.

- Spread bet: Short at 46. Target 35. Stop 55.

This looked a goodie: Yell is of course famous for directories, but with the internet taking over and big debt of £4.1bn it looked a good short.

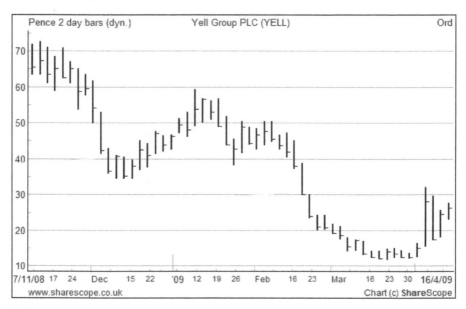

Yell

I was in for £75 a point. From 46 it just kept on going down. It easily went through the first target so I held on, and on, and on, and eventually I exited at 16 for a profit of £2250 (30 x 75).

This was on the basis that if it went bust I'd only have a few points left to gain anyway but chances were there would be some kind of fundraising to keep it afloat.

Aero Inventory

A great short that I didn't put on but wish I had!

I looked at Aero Inventory and so nearly put on a short. Initially I was thinking of it as a buy as profits had risen so much, but it also showed a massive debt of more than £400m, which looked way too high. Especially compared to the (relatively) small profits being made. Not only that – as you can see, the shares had topped out and were reversing nicely.

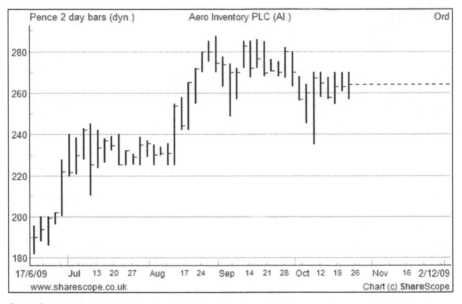

Aero Inventory

The price when I was debating whether to short was around 270. Two weeks later the company's shares were suspended, and soon after that it when into administration. Which means I would have collected 270 times my stake.

Arrrgggghhhhh!

It's hard when you miss out. However, if you had been long of this share you would have LOST 270 times your stake. Ouch. So you should think carefully before buying shares with huge debt. It is asking for trouble. Be careful.

DEBT NOTE: Check my website for details about how I look for debt and work out it might be too high. In a nutshell: a net debt of more than three times full-year pre-tax profits to me is too high. That's because I noticed that in the past companies had gone bust with 5x, so 3x looks a good safety net.

NOTE: If you are involved with any of the companies I have written about and I got anything wrong with your figures or I upset you by shorting it then I'm really sorry. What I did is in the past now. Please don't be cross.

FTSE 100 shorts

I've done pretty well with these over the years. I tend to try and have one or two on when the markets are in decline and, in general, had some open during the big bear declines of 2000-2002 and 2008-2009. Shrewd traders realise the FTSE has in effect moved sideways for many years – it's a matter of catching some of the ride as it trends up and down, even though nothing much is really happening over multiple years.

Let's start with my 2010 one.

As you can see from the chart, in early 2010 the FTSE 100 had recovered well after the bear market, but at the beginning of the year it tried a number of times to rise above 5500 – and just couldn't. This looked like an excellent time to short and I went in for a fiver at 5489, targeting somewhere around 5000 where it has found support a couple of times.

FTSE 100

The idea here was to cut it quick if it went wrong – I'd have been out at 5550, which would have been a breakout. As it happens, at the time of writing this trade is still open at 5500 and well in the money!

Going back in time to the bear market, I managed to get shorts in at around 6600 – the market topped out twice at about 6800. I then generally had a short open all the way down to the high 3000s where it bottomed out.

After that I left the FTSE alone as a short until it reached much higher levels and began to run out of steam.

One lesson learned was that I did quite a few trades when I'd have actually made more money by sticking with one or two shorts for six months or more – instead, I kept taking profits and then getting back in. However, that is with hindsight, which is of course a wonderful thing.

To summarise: the best time to short is when you can see that the share, index, etc has hit the same area time and time again and won't rise above it – i.e. when it's resisting. This is the time to get in. But also keep a close eye. See Man Group.

Conversely, just because I don't generally do FTSE upbets there is nothing to stop you doing them if you want to. Here, I would do the opposite and look for when the FTSE tries a few times to fall below a certain point but can't (support). So there is your probable entry!

Before I move on to some long-trade examples here are some…

Shorting tips in brief

- Please remember to sell and not buy! When closing a short, buy, or press 'close'.

- Think short-term (a few days to around a month).

- Don't try and short a strong riser or try and guess a new trend.

- Look to short weak companies with big debt or in a losing sector.

- Don't try and short strong companies with big profits and lots of cash.

- Close for a small loss fast if you get it wrong.

- Set a target but stick with the trade if it sinks through.

- See if you can use support and resistance.

- Stick to your stop loss!

Okay, that's a few shorts done and dusted, so now let's look at some long trades. Remember: 'long' is jargon for betting on a share or index to go up.

Long trades

Firstly, I want to explain why I bother long-trading shares using spread betting at all. After all, once you take the extra spread into account there isn't that much in it cost-wise between spread betting and buying shares tax-free in an ISA.

- I spread bet if it's an AIM rather than a main market share. That's because you can't put AIM shares into an ISA – trading them via spread betting retains tax-free status for your profits.

- I spread bet if something is moving quickly and I want to get in fast. Usually it's quicker to press the spread-bet button than to buy the shares.

- I also spread bet if my ISA is fully invested or simply to top up on a share I like on a more short-term basis.

Gottit? Right then. That's just me, of course. You might look at spread betting differently.

Oh, and I should add that I tend to only go long on spread bets if the general market is trending up.

Okay then, some long trades...

Avanti Communications

- Reason: A technology AIM share with big potential.

- Spread bet: Long at 340. Target 550. Stop 300.

I bought this for £20 a point with a longer-term view, so I bought it on a nine-month expiry paying a little more on the spread. I felt its satellite technology promised potentially explosive growth.

The chart isn't an awful lot of use with this one, as it has a wide spread and moves fast.

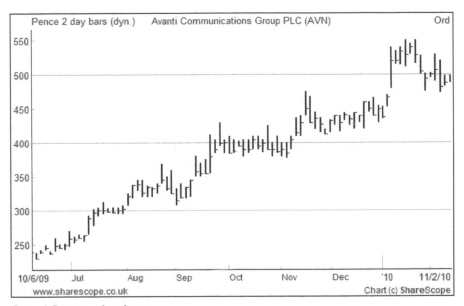

Avanti Communications

But it's an amazing looking, strong chart and a share just crying out to be bought. If it had had a full listing I would probably have bought it in the standard way. It was hard to set my target. Of course, as a tech share it carries a fair degree of risk, but for exposure of about £7k I thought it was worth it. In fact, I still hold it as I write this and the shares have touched 500 – a profit of over £3000 so far (160 x 20). I am currently tempted to take profits, as 500 looks like it could prove a major resistance point.

Centamin

- Reason: A volatile commodity stock to trade quickly!

- Spread bet: Long at 110. Target 130. Stop 106

I like to have the odd share that's volatile so I can get to know its pattern; where it gets bought and where it gets sold. A bit like the earlier Wolseley short.

Centamin's a smaller commodity stock that seems to repeat its movements – so I enjoyed playing it for short-term gains from time to time. This is one share I played on the long side rather than short.

Why's that?

Because I'd worry about being short of a commodity stock where an announcement could come out about a find of some value – in which case a short could be quickly demolished.

Take a look at the chart and see how it ranges between 108 and about 140 – when it moves one way it tends to keep that trend for a few days. My plan was simply to buy at the support area at around 110 and sell up to 140 – allowing it to turn a little downwards first.

Centamin

So I made quite a few small trades, most of which worked out – usually lasting from one day or two, to a week. The point here is if you can find a stock like this – and you're careful and follow the trend – you can pick up a load of wins.

The other beauty of this share, as I write, is if it can break through the sticky 140 area, there could be a nice up lift from 140 to 170 and then possibly a new 140-170 trend to play for a while. My last trade in this was at 110, and my target of 130 was hit for a £20 a point profit.

Of course not every trade in this share will be a winner, but if I made a trade and it fell then I'd get out fast. So if I bought at 110 and it fell below 106, where 108 had been support, I'd exit fast with a small loss.

Afren

- Reason: Promising oil stock with lovely trading ranges.
- Spread bet: Long at 84.5. Target 97.50. Stop 76.

Afren

Take a look at the chart and see the sensational trading range that always bottoms at 80, or just below. Can you see how many times it does that? This made it a lovely easy short-term buy for me in the low 80s. So I kept buying anywhere in the 80-85 range, selling at where it always tops out, either at 95 or just above 100. Once a range like this has been established it literally is as easy as buying at 80ish every time. Again, I don't short on the way down because a news event such as a discovery could suddenly push a share like this much higher. Plus it's currently in a long-term uptrend.

I made a number of decent bets on this share. One example would be a buy for £50 at 84.5, near the bottom of the range, exiting at 97.50 near the top of the range for a profit of £650 (13 x 50).

Burren Energy

My best spread bet ever!

- Reason: A new issue that appeared promising and to which I wanted extra exposure.

- Spread bet: Long at 260. Target 350. Stop 220.

This one is going back in time but I bought £20 a point in oil company Burren Energy at 260p. It was a new listing and I spread bet on it in addition to a normal share buy.

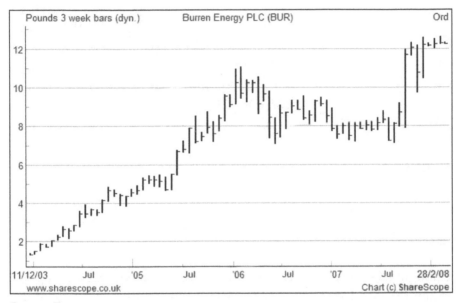

Burren Energy

I hadn't intended to hold the bet for very long, but the thing is, it just kept on going up! Every time it dipped a bit and I felt like taking profits, it began to rise again. So I just left it going. I decided to sell it when it got to around 1000, only for a takeover bid for it to be made at 1230! That gave me a gain of 970 points x £20, or £19,400!

Every time the bet was due to expire I just rolled over. Of course this did cost me a bit in spread every time, so in fairness I would guess all the rollovers cost me about £1000. With this trade there was a fair bit of luck involved, but it shows that sometimes a spread bet can be hung onto for a long time. It happens about once a year for me. So, just sometimes, if it keeps going up, then hold on!

Dimension Data

- Reason: Great rising profits, good sector.

- Spread bet: Long at 67. Target 100. Stop 62.

I went big on this and bought for £200 at 67; that's exposure of over £13,000. Not a decision I took lightly!

Dimension Data

I bought this to add more exposure to the share, which I already had in my ISA. As I write I'm yet to close it out, and it's at 80 yielding a nice profit. You can also see the powerful uptrend in the chart. My plan would be to gradually start to sell some and take profits at just under 100 (round numbers, like 100, can be difficult for prices to break through).

Micro Focus

- Reason: Amazing trading update, top up as my ISA was fully invested.

- Spread bet: Long at 387. Target 500. Stop 350.

Micro Focus

A really strong 'ahead of expectations' statement got me into this one at £20 a point. It was also rising powerfully at my time of entry, as you can see from the chart. It kept on rising and went through my target, so I then raised the stop loss to 500. This proved a good move as it started to fall back and I got taken out at 496 for a profit of £2180 (109 x 20). The price was coming down because a news statement was due the following day.

StatPro

- Reason: Excellent share in major upturn.

- Spread bet: Long at 101. Target 150. Stop 90.

I traded StatPro as a spread bet because it's an AIM stock. I bought for £50 a point and it was hard to set a stop or target because it just kept on rising (and so there were no significant support or resistance levels). So, as usual, I set a stop of 10% but the sky was the limit in terms of target. I bought this with a longer-term view so bought the spread on an expiry some nine months away. Sometimes one can go into a trade with the idea of holding for the longer-term.

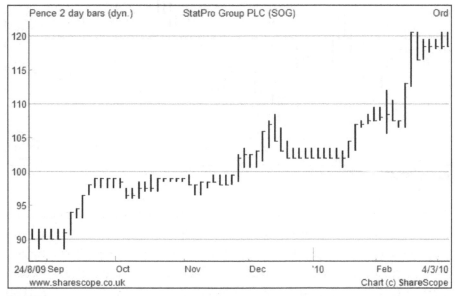

StatPro

At the time of writing I still hold this bet (the price is currently at 120), with the view of taking a part profit at 150. Well, that's if it should get there! If it got to 130 and started sliding then I would probably raise the stop to 115 to protect the profit.

Small oil shares and spread betting!

Remember I've been talking about the tax-free bit of spread betting quite a bit? It's especially good if you, like me, occasionally strike it big with an oil tiddler!

What I mean by strike it big is that, once in a while, a long spread bet on an oil minor that subsequently finds oil can secure a big tax-free win. For example, if you'd been lucky enough to be in on one of the small oil companies that struck oil in the Falkland Islands in 2010, your spread bet could have ended up being worth a fortune.

Say you had bought a speculative £200 a point in Rockhopper when it was 20p – that's £4000 worth of exposure.

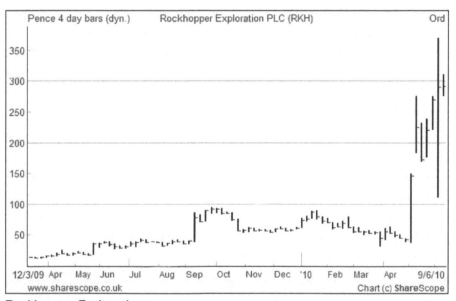

Rockhopper Exploration

Look at what happened! You could have sold at 350 for a profit of £66,000 – all tax free! Outside a spread bet there would have been a capital gains tax bill of over £20,000 to pay. Look at how much you saved by spread betting it!

A number of very small oil shares did very well in 2010 – and every year there are usually at least one or two that sprout wings. Of course, for every small oiler that does well there's one that doesn't! It's a matter of really doing some research into the area in which they are drilling and trying to figure out their chances of finding oil. The market tends to give some clues – if you are in one and it starts to trickle down, it might be worth getting out. If you see a lot of sell trades, there's a clue something isn't right.

If, on the other hand, you see lots of buys coming in and the price lifting – that could be a clue to get in!

Encore, encore!

One small oiler I've bought is EnCore Oil, staking £300 a point at 28p after it announced a discovery of oil in the North Sea. That announcement was enough to get my interest! £300 a point is the equivalent of about eight grands' worth of exposure. (Of course, now you've read most of this book, you could already work that out, couldn't you?)

Often, once a discovery is made by an oil company, it can be followed by others. The share price ends up going even higher. However, sometimes there are follow up announcements that turn out to be not so good. Maybe there wasn't as much oil as hoped, or it wasn't of good enough quality. At the time of writing this, EnCore has made another decent announcement and is up at 45p, giving a paper profit of ... anyone? ... £5100 (45 - 28 x 300).

I would now start to move the stop loss up under the price to seal in profits. The discovery on this company simply came from looking in the papers; research was easy and I thought it worth the gamble.

Being crude

There are dangers and delights in having one or two small oil gambles. These of course revolve around drilling updates!

Get a good one at 7am and have a great day! Get a bad one and you may be scrambling to get out.

My view is to immediately write off 70% of any stake and treat any profits as a bonus. In other words, don't go crazy and put everything you have into a small oil stock. Because over a week they can climb 50% on good news, and they can equally fall 50% on bad.

If you do spread bet one of these, remember you will be paying a wider spread with a spread bet firm and the spread will already probably be large – so it might be worth going for a long expiry bet to give it a chance without running up rolling bet costs.

The main thing, also, is to do as much research as you can on these high-risk stocks and don't take too much notice of bulletin board posters!

I hope some of my real-life trades have given you a flavour of how I do my spread betting – it's a mixture, I think, of common sense, the chart, fundamentals and (legal) tax avoidance!

11. Traders' Tales

I thought it would be a good idea to invite people who had recently started spread betting to tell me how they got on and whether it was a good or bad experience.

I was inundated with stories and I've picked out ones that represent the major things that have gone wrong (or right) for people. They are worth a read because these true stories might stop you from making a terrible mistake. There are some good hints and tips contained within the stories. And also – let's be perfectly honest here – there is nothing like reading about other people's balls-ups!

I've also added a comment or two to each story.

So I suggest you run yourself a nice bath, put lots of bubble bath in, relax and enjoy these true stories.

But please make sure you don't drop the book in the ba...Oh dear... Too late. Let it dry on the radiator, and see you in crumpled form later...

I thought I was being clever

Colin's tale:

❝ I had seven trades open in the US market – all short. I thought I was being clever analysing by sector and identifying and shorting a couple of the big real-estate companies that were in a strong downtrend.

Day one, all trades were making profits until half an hour before market close when the market started rising. The day closed in negative territory on all my open positions. Then I got an email article from one of the *MoneyWeek* magazine writers talking of a possible US stock-market bounce, which happened on opening the next session.

I have to say I got spooked and saw all my positions gradually lose even more money. I tried not to keep looking at the trades during the day in case I prematurely closed any down and there was a reversal. Next day I lost my nerve as all were losing positions, so I closed them all out at a loss.

I'm not sure I did the wrong thing here, as they all would have hit their stops for even greater losses; however, I did not feel very disciplined. **""**

NT comments:

Well, on this occasion the fact you panicked helped you! But normally you ought to trade your plan. It sounds like your stops could have been too far away. Also, you ended up trading against a new trend.

Panic as losses mount up

Hosk's tale:

"" This is a story about my first day spread betting.

I bet on the FTSE going down. At the time everything was going down, so it seemed a good bet. I watched the charts and saw that it was moving to a certain pattern, bouncing up and down in a nice predictable way.

I patiently waited until it got to the top of the wave and then put my short bet on, but instead of a cash bet I put it on as a bet for the quarter.

I watched with glee as the FTSE went down and my profit went up. Fantastic! The only thing I could complain about was I bet only £1 a point. I then put a cash bet on for a higher amount. This was easy money and I had a chance to get more, so I placed the bet for £5 a point.

Then I saw it was coming to the bottom of the wave and I wanted to get out and take a nice profit. Hmmm, how do you stop the spread bet?

I tried buying the bet only for nothing to happen, aargghhhh…Or did something happen? Wait a minute – I put a stop loss on my first bet, do I have to cancel that first? How do you cancel a stop loss?

I pressed *buy* on the cash bet, nothing happened.

The FTSE was going up, nonononoooo. I could see the loss piling up, it was 35, 45, 60. Help, I'm trapped! The money is falling out of my account every second. I was looking on the website for instructions but, bah, nothing.

Then my boss came over to my desk to talk about some bug in the software. "*Bug in the software*! You should see this spread betting site, it won't let me cancel my bet and I'm losing money at an alarming rate." I didn't say that but I wanted to. I minimised my screen, trying to pay attention and get rid of my boss as quickly as possible.

Finally, after what seemed like hours, but was only one minute, he left. I looked at the screen and I was £100 down on the second bet and even down on the first.

I finally got out of the trades and sat back startled and sweating – and bloody relieved I still had some money in my account. **99**

NT comments:

A brilliant cautionary tale from Hosk. Two things really: first you must understand how to close out a spread bet with the firm you choose. This might mean putting on a few small trades first to check everything goes smoothly, before you place bigger bets.

Secondly, Hosk was trading from work! Be careful on volatile bets if you can't get access to your screen at crucial times – for instance because your boss might come round the corner and you'll have to take the spread betting firm off your terminal fast!

My stop was still active!

Phil's tale:

66 I followed advice and opened a number of spread betting accounts, the reason being to search around and get the best spread. Over a period of months I wasn't as keen on a couple of the companies for various reasons and didn't use them for a while. It was only after constantly receiving an email statement from one of the companies that I thought, "Why do they keep sending these when I have no open trades with them?" I investigated and found that I'd closed a trade out about six weeks before and took my profit, which was a short. However, plonker me didn't cancel the stop loss and the trade rose and hit the stop, which opened a long trade that I was oblivious to.

Very luckily the share continued to rise giving me a profit of over £300 for £2 a point. Although this ridiculous situation worked out OK, *always cancel the stop when closing out a trade.* **99**

NT comments:

Phil's story is quite common. Always ensure you really have closed out a bet (including stops). Don't forget that stop orders can be used to open positions – not just close them. With some companies you must ensure your stop loss is cancelled alongside the bet. So check your accounts carefully every day to ensure everything is as it should be.

Horror of spread betting the indices

David's tale:

" Over a week, I tried to bet on the FTSE going up and down. It's a terrible game. Almost as soon as I bought a bet the stupid FTSE would then reverse direction and instantly start losing me money, then all I would be hoping for would be to get out even or sell quick before I lost any more.

When I tried this darting-in tactic on shares, I was like a direction-change magnet. Almost to the second the share would change direction. I must have been the last person to join the herd of others shorting a share. The share price would react as if a small 'idiot spread bettor' alarm had gone off and it'd change direction the instant I pressed the buy or sell button.

I have now learnt: don't start spread betting without a plan. Research, research, research, wait for the right time and then place your bet and write this down either in a journal or an Excel spreadsheet so you can learn from your failures and successes. Don't waste your failures. Not losing money is almost as good as making money. You have to look after it because without money you can't place any more bets. "

NT comments:

A great contribution from David. His best comment is "Don't start spread betting without a plan". A plan of some kind – any kind – is a must. Trying to make quick money out of betting on the FTSE is doomed to failure unless you are really, really good, and 90% of traders lose at this. Think carefully before going down this avenue.

A point a day

Chris's tale:

" Having done some research on the internet about the subject of spread betting, I was sold on the idea! The fact that you could use the leverage available to improve your earning potential sounded great, and the tax advantages were too good to pass up.

I had £1500 that I deposited into an online spread betting account. If I lost this money it wouldn't be the end of the world for me, although I would be in the doghouse with my fiancée for a while (it's part of our wedding fund!).

From my research, I was very much aware of the need to have a plan. So I decided to put one together.

Being a bit of a novice, I decided that I should keep it simple. I was looking for quick returns, and having looked at a few charts I decided on a system that couldn't possibly fail. The plan was to make just a single point (after spreads) of profit per day. Looking at some charts, it seemed perfectly easy to do this – all you have to do is wait for something to go down a bit, then when it gets to the bottom, bet that it'll come up a bit!

Each day, I would bet 1/30th of my total pot per point. So – on the first day I would be betting £50 per point of my £1500 pot. By simply catching a 1-point per day movement, this system would grow my account by over 3% per day! This would turn my £1500 into £30,000 in about 100 days – and all by winning trades of just 1 point!

Whilst being quite sceptical of my plan, I'm also an optimistic and inquisitive kind of person, so I set about the task of running my system!

The good news is that it worked! After 12 days of trading I had doubled my money and had a pot of £3000 – a target which, according to the original plan, I wouldn't get to for another 11 days! I did most of my trading first thing in the morning. Most days I had finished trading for the day by 8.30am, with trades open sometimes for less than a minute!

Then, on the 13th day, things didn't quite go according to plan and I lost £675 – a massive 22.5% of my pot! I wasn't happy, but then everyone has a bad day – I thought. So I pressed on for the next four days, making £99 but losing another £375.

One of the things that I did right was to keep an accurate log of all of my trades. This meant that I could quite clearly see that what was once working for me was working no more! I decided to take a break to try and see what was going wrong.

Looking at the charts over the period that I traded, it would seem that the share I was dealing was range-bound for the first couple of weeks. Unbeknownst to me, it was the share price bouncing between resistance and support that was making it so easy to predict the movement. It was on the 13th day that the share broke out of this range and started behaving more erratically, and all of a sudden a simple 1-point movement wasn't so easy to predict!

I started to make what I now know to be all of the classic mistakes. I was letting my losses run in the hope that they would turn around. I snatched at profits, often closing earlier than I needed too. When I made a loss on a long, I sometimes immediately went short – chasing my losses. If only I had known about "tea and toast days" then.

So – I have (for now) abandoned this particular style of trading. I have still made over £500 profit in a very short space of time, so I'm still very happy – but now I am looking at the companies I trade in much more detail. I am planning my *trades* rather than just my *profit target*. I am now planning to have trades that will hopefully last for between a week and a month, with planned stops and targets. **99**

NT comments:

I think Chris sums up his story himself: he was planning profit targets and not trades. He also got emotionally involved, immediately going the opposite way on a trade that had already lost. You can lose a lot of money this way. Also, chasing a small amount of points is usually a bad plan and ends up with snatched profits and lots of losers. Learn from this story!

Large bets to compensate for losers

Keith's tale:

66 I started spread betting about six months ago, with little knowledge and pretty much just learning by losing.

I thought it was a great system as it allowed me to place bets on shares and indices without very much capital and it looked like a straightforward method for making good money quickly.

I also thought I would set very tight stop losses to keep me safe in this supposedly dangerous game. The problem with this was even if a share was moving up over the period of a day or two, I would have been knocked out of the game by a very short-term price drop. The next problem I experienced was putting larger bets on to try and compensate for the previous losses. Not a good idea! Finally, I also bought into Lloyds Group (regular shares) when they were much higher than they are currently and I guess the old emotional attachment to the share happened to me. I would continually bet both long and short on this share in an attempt to try and profit something from it. Needless to say, that did not happen!

Currently I am down over £500 on spread betting alone, and have decided to learn more about both share trading and spread betting before I go back into it! **99**

NT comments:

Several common mistakes highlighted here by Keith. Putting on bigger bets to try and get back losses is a no-no. Don't! It will lead to bigger losses. Setting tight stop losses on volatile shares is a bad idea too – you could lose on every bet on a morning spike down. Getting emotionally involved with one share will also lead to losses. Three things to avoid here, as Keith realised.

Lessons learned from three months of spread betting

Denis's tale:

❝ I have been spread betting the markets for approx three months now so I'm a novice.

I have taken it easy and only traded approx 15 times with no more than two trades open at any one time. My trades have been small at £1 a point and so far I have made a small profit of £142.

If I was going to put forward some pointers for anyone new to spread betting I would include the following:

- When you see spread betting, see *fire*. If you understand fire you know you can use it to enrich your life, but if you're not concentrating or you play with it you'll get burnt!

- Start off with a demo account until you understand how spread betting works. Once you are happy to move on to the real thing I would start trading at £1 per point. Trading with real money is totally different to a demo account; your mind will behave differently when there is money at stake, so it is best to start small.

- Be aware of the spread. With smaller companies especially, your trade might have to do a fair bit of work just to get it to a level position.

- If you find yourself glued to the screen watching every tick up and down then maybe spread betting is not for you. Do your research, put your trade on and let it get to work.

- *Set stop losses!* As soon as you make a trade, check the stop loss and adjust it to a place you feel comfortable. If it hits this point and you are stopped out then be pleased you protected your capital and *don't go chasing your losses*.

- If the trade goes well move the stop loss in the direction of the trade, locking in some of the profits. It's a great feeling securing profits as the trade goes the way you thought.

- *Beware indices!* These things move fast. If you're not prepared and are out of your depth you will lose heavily.

- SB is an excellent trading tool when used in the right way. I would urge every private investor to research its benefits and to try it out. There are lots of great deals available at the moment. Why not make use of them and learn the ropes with someone else's money? **99**

NT comments:

I don't have much to add to Denis' advice here because he is spot on with all of it! Digest and learn.

A shorting delight

Wayne's tale:

66 My first dabble was shorting the Dow and I won £46. A good start!

Taking your advice, after doing some research and finding that I was most certainly in agreement with you, I bet on Next at 1221.4 for the vast sum of £3 a point. Sweating and with heart racing, it began to go down. I eventually bought the next day at 1112.6, netting me a profit of £326.40. I was ecstatic, and the neighbours thought I had finally gone over the edge when I began running around the garden whooping like a demented Red Indian!

Since then, I've been in and out of the Dow, shorting on each occasion for a short period of time – I'm talking about minutes – and making a small profit on each trade. I must admit though that the Next short, perhaps because it was my first, got the pulse racing, heart pounding and sweat pouring. (I haven't experienced that for a *very* long time!)

My advice, for what it's worth, is to only use small sums initially. Spread betting is great fun, but potentially dangerous. If it starts to go against you, get out fast. **99**

NT comments:

Wayne was shorting while the market was going down in a recession. What it shows is that you must remember with spread betting that you can bet on shares to go up *or* down. Next was a good idea for a short as retailers were being hammered at the time. I would add, though, that shorting can be very dangerous in an uptrend. Always understand which way the market is trending and try and go with it.

Went bust trading indices

Clarence's tale:

" To fit with my day job I was attracted to trading the DOW as it's open in the evening. This led to a few heavy losses but was partially balanced by some wins. This continued for six months. The account was started with £1500 as this was initially needed for margin on the share trades, but on reflection this gave me too high a level of comfort for a novice trading the indexes. Soon this account was effectively bust and I needed a new strategy.

Now along the way I had learnt a lot and had been keeping a good record of my trades so I could analyse success and failure. Upon review it was clear that I knew enough to get it right, in a small way, and was learning more about technical analysis. But I was weak on exiting losing trades. The price you pay for education! My conclusion was I needed a more disciplined approach and a much smaller account size, to force caution. This runs contrary to popular advice as a 1% or 2% risk of bank per trade is considered optimal (that, however, assumes the discipline of stops).

Stops – automatic or mental – are another psychological dilemma and another demon to control. From my research on websites and bulletin boards I uncovered a body of opinion that suggested SB companies trade against you and deliberately spike to take out stops. When I used auto stops I thought I saw this as some trades soon turned around and went to profit, leaving me with a loss at the point of maximum pain. Much of this I later concluded to be the usual trader error of seeing what you're looking for and not what is there. Many of my losses were down to letting losers run while I waited for the market to turn, only to ultimately reach a point where the size and pain of loss was even greater. "

NT comments:

Letting losers run and hoping they correct is one of the bigger mistakes. "Seeing what you are looking for and not what is there" is a great comment and so true.

Lost £10,000 betting on house prices

Andy's tale:

" This story should make you cringe, and still makes my blood boil, but hopefully passing on my experience will stop somebody else making similar mistakes.

This story has the lot: inexperience, overconfidence, trading with money I couldn't afford to lose, bad timing, greed, panic and products I didn't understand.

In 2005, having watched the UK housing market like a hawk and deciding not to join the first-time-buyers stampede, I sat on the side lines and waited for the market to crash.

I did a serious amount of research and predicted the top of the market in April 2005. Having the knowledge of this market, my next question was, "How can I profit from this, apart from by buying a cheaper house?"

A spread firm was running bets – and probably still is – on London house prices. I opted to short the market at £250k, at something like £250 per point.

All was well and the market ticked down. I even waited a while to let the market move south before entering my trade so I was moving with the trend. Or so I thought!

Profits came quickly and I was feeling like a bit of a hero, and so I quickly added to my position and took out another short at £125 per point.

As the second trade slipped into profit, I then took a third and was now in big time at a total of £500 per point. But I was going to make a fortune, or at least enough to put down a serious deposit on my first house!

I think I was about £3000 up when the market went dead, it just stopped moving. I left it a week, then two, and then contacted the spread firm. They said: "We have closed the market as we can't fill positions and plan to re-open the book in a few months." I didn't think any more of it.

Some time later I got a phone call, they wanted some more cash, and quickly. This was to keep me alive in my trade. I battled on the phone saying, "This can't be true, you have closed the books, and I was making money when you were last open." The reply was, "We have now re-opened the books and it has gapped up as the housing market has risen."

It was now trading at £268k to sell.

Before, the market had been moving around one point a week.

Panic hit me like never before. This was completely out of the blue. I was literally spinning and really couldn't focus on anything. This was a serious amount of money; hours passed before I got myself together and planned to just get out before this could really destroy everything.

The market had closed by this time, so I had the night to plan (believe it or not I even thought of averaging down, but fortunately I came to my senses).

I woke early and closed out as soon as the market opened. I felt free and relieved to be out, but the market had moved another two points up, which made me close out at £270k – a 20-point loss at £500 per point.

Total loss of £10k.

I complained to the FSA and ombudsman about the spread firm opening and shutting markets when they felt like it, but I had no joy. Apparently they were within their rights to do so.

It really, really hit me hard that I had thrown away our house deposit. I can't believe I lost it betting, which is something I thought I'd never do! I remember at the time it didn't seem like betting – it all seemed very logical, practical and intelligent.

Perhaps I was naïve, perhaps I was unlucky or perhaps I was just ahead of the times! **"**

NT comments:

Well Andy, maybe a mix of all three! You were unlucky that the market was suspended – if a market is unusual, like house prices, check with the firm concerned how liquid the market is and beware of putting too much on.

Check your trades if something seems totally wrong

Paul's tale:

" I'd placed (via the net) a trade before the market opened on Brent Oil to fall over the day. The day before the price had been quite strong and I felt certain there would be some profit taking. Anyway, on returning a few hours later the screen was showing a huge loss! I went into a state of sheer panic and called the spread firm. I can't recall the conversation very well, but it started something like:

"I don't know what the f**k I meant to do, but I didn't think I'd lose so much. Help!"

All the time, I was certain that I'd set up and executed this trade properly. I'm watching the screen and it's driving away from me into a bigger loss. I'd lost my mind. And then the phone rang; it was the SB company again. Only this time a different chap! He'd been trying to get in touch with me all morning, as they had put the trade on at the wrong entry point and had been trying to exit without loss (to them) since. In my relief, I asked him to reverse the position and put me back to my starting point prior to the trade; which he duly did. If I'd have remained calmer, I would have realised that I should have told him to put me in at the actual position that I had originally requested.

Moral of the story – don't panic if things don't seem in order! Always check and make a note of your trades! **"**

NT comments:

Sometimes this happens and the spread firm get an entry price wrong. Always check your account and check the price! Sometimes a wrong trade or someone else's trade may appear in your account – always phone the company right away!

£2200 to £220 in four days

Chris's tale:

" I opened two SB accounts. With one I traded equities and managed to grow £350 into £2200 in two months by applying TA strategies.

With the other I traded the FTSE and while I had some initial success I got overconfident and consequently emotional when the bets went against me.

I made this worse by increasing my bet size to recoup losses, feeling sure the market would swing back, or alternatively I would reverse my strategy, which inevitably led to the market doing a u-turn. It felt like the market knew what I was up to and was having a laugh at my expense. This then brought in fear of loss so I set stop losses, but I set them too tight for the average expected fluctuation. I quickly zeroed out this account and decided that betting on the indices is just gambling.

Unfortunately, with the equities account, I again got confident and greedy through success and started to use bet sizes beyond what was reasonable for my account size. This of course led to bigger losses and again, through the need to recoup those losses, I put new large bets on after my stop losses had been hit.

Consequently my £2200 went to £220 in the space of four days.

Several hundred of this was lost by 8am market adjustments spiking through my stops/limits and some smaller losses by day-trading volatile stocks.

I decided to set myself some strict rules:

- Never go straight back into a bet if a stop loss has been hit.

- Have a good reason for placing the bet and stick to my stop/limit strategy.

- Protect my capital – don't put bet sizes on that could result in losses of more than 10% of my account (to be revised as account grows).

- Be aware of 8am market adjustment spikes when setting stops/limits.

I also have a guideline never to bet on the same stock twice in the same week to give me a better chance of following a trend.

I'm doing better now, choosing bets based on minimal potential losses and big potential gains, e.g. I gained £600 on a £1 spread with a stop loss set at -£50 (which I quickly moved to zero once the bet was heading in the right direction). **99**

NT comments:

Some excellent rules to finish off that story. I love never betting on the same one twice in one week – it is too easy to get emotionally attached to one stock and want to have revenge on that share.

Know your trading platform

David's tale:

66 For a while I was using and testing a variety of platforms to see which I liked best. What you find is that not all platforms are the same and you need to make sure you understand the differences.

For example, some platforms work fine when I log on at home, but if I log on at work I have signal quality and connectivity problems. I am not a techie so I am not sure why this is the case.

With one or two firms, if you open a trade together with a related stop order then it is worth noting that the stop order will not be cancelled automatically should you close the initial trade. For example, I was trading PV Crystalox Solar (PVCS) and thought its price would rise, so I went £20 a point on the price to rise. At the same time my protective stop-loss order was put in place to sell PVCS should it move against me and fall to my stop loss price.

Initially all went to plan, the price rose and I closed out the position at a small profit. The next time I logged in, imagine my surprise when I noticed I was making a loss on PVCS. I didn't understand how this could be until I noticed that PVCS had fallen in price, activating my stop-loss order, and had then started to rise in price again. The stop loss hadn't been cancelled when I closed my initial trade. I effectively had an unwanted open position at £20 for PVCS to fall in price when it was rising. I immediately closed the position.

What was really annoying is that the loss outweighed my earlier gain and it was caused by a lack of platform understanding and concentration. I should have spotted this by just checking my account's funding requirement, which would have signalled that I had a margin exposure.

In short, find a platform you like and get to know all its little quirks, reliability and functionality. **"**

NT comments:

Excellent story. I agree it is always worth trying a few different companies to see which suits best. And especially beware if using one where you have to cancel the stop as well as close the trade. And always check your open positions.

Thought I was a genius

Charles's tale:

" A few years ago I hit a great streak on indices and currencies in a roaring bull market; I felt like a genius who could do no wrong. I turned a small £500 account into almost £2000 in a few months – small feed but a useful experiment for me. At this rate I was going to be a billionaire in a few years!

I then started increasing the leverage. I went from 50p a-point bets to around £2 a point. When it all went south, as it did very quickly – a 75% loss in about three days from three positions – the extent of my recklessness became clear. I had three currency positions open, each at close to four times larger than what I was used to (i.e. 50p up to around £6/point). The currencies were all correlated and there were major announcements coming out that made big moves happen. I was long and wrong and the psychological knock bothers me to this day. I have a mental block that I need to overcome – a magic number I need to break through. I will always wonder where my account would be now if I had made those trades a winner and doubled the account again.

To this day my problems are trading products too volatile and expensive for my trading account, slow small winners and rapid big losers. I'll keep paying my fees to Mr Market until I start to learn from my mistakes. **"**

NT comments:

A big problem with spread betting accounts. A few wins with small stakes can make traders overconfident – they then go whacking in big bets to suddenly find it all changes. One spread firm I talked to said one new trader came in and made £150,000 profit quickly – a week later the same trader was losing £50,000! Beware of bigger stakes than you can afford, or feeling you are better than Mr Market.

Bet too much

Steve's tale:

" I started having some punts (that's what they were back then) and first tried betting on the FTSE 100 index. Bad idea. Didn't have the nerves for it and lost some money. Not loads, but after a few bad bets I was £100 down.

I made some spread bets on companies like Barclays, but bet too much and got too involved emotionally, following daily-trends up and down and betting, trying to take a few quid here and there. It was exhausting!

Instead of spread betting, however, I'm going to concentrate on buying shares and dealing with investments for a year, and then add spread betting to my skill set after that.

If you want to try spread betting, I recommend you open several different accounts with around £100 in each, and try them out, side-by-side to see which you like and why. Things to compare:

- spreads
- whether you can actually get the bet you want (such as betting on futures – where you can bet on a price three or six months away)
- if the spread betting firm closes out bets
- whether they support automated stops.

You may well find that one system works with you, while you feel that others are working against you. Learn from my mistakes! **"**

NT comments:

Steve is right! Spread betting should be in addition to other investments. Also, betting on daily indices is very difficult and brain-destroying!

Lost trading against the trend

Dan's tale:

66 I've been trading for just over two and a half years, and about six months ago I started spread betting. When I first started trading I did it with the view that I was young (28 at the time) and didn't have lots of money in the bank, but all going well I felt I could add to my savings.

The concepts in your book *The Naked Trader* made sense so I set about investing, but thinking I knew best I did it by breaking almost every rule in your book. My favourite idea was to look out for a share that had just had bad news, wait for it to drop before buying it, and then watch it rise. It worked occasionally to start with, but then I started losing a lot more than I made. Basically I wanted to make money very quickly (within a few hours!). I now approach investing completely differently.

Anyway I tell you this because I started my spread betting in exactly the same way. I would look at the chart and think, "That's gone up or down too far, it must go the other way soon," and I would bet against the trend. Problem was, even if I was right I'd get out almost as soon as I started losing money. In the end I made a lot of small losses. I decided to take a step back and change my approach. At the time the pound was very weak against the euro and I believed it would rise so I set myself a stop loss of 400 pips and placed my bet. At first the euro continued to rise and I was about 140 pips down before it turned in my favour. I closed my position over 400 pips up. Since then I only bet on something I believe will happen long/medium term and I give the position a chance to prove my speculation correct or not. I set myself a stop loss so I can only lose what I set out prepared to lose.

I don't regret losing any of the money I have lost spread betting or buying/selling shares as I see it as a valuable lesson; and I at least managed to stick to one rule and not risk more than I could afford to lose. 99

NT comments:

Excellent, glad you learnt from your mistakes. Trading against the trend is the path to selling *The Big Issue*. Same comment with trying to make money too quickly. Greed often leads to big losses.

Learning to forget emotion when trading

Phil's tale:

❝ What I was interested in was something for the partner. Her health isn't great and doing even a part-time job is a bit of a challenge. She only gets about £70 a week and, I can't believe it, she does voluntary work with the elderly too. Respect. Anyway, I saw a few of these FOREX systems that offered the prospect of replacing her salary with little risk.

I tried [System XYZ. – Ed] first and it didn't work. No problem, I got my money back. Another system looked to have better legs. I tried it and found it seemed to be better and so I showed her the mechanics, which she picked up fairly easily. We set up an account and got her paper trading. It all started very well with a few losses but a lot more wins. She had £2000 in a pot that she felt she could risk. As soon as she traded live the reverse happened, not many wins and lots of losses. Eventually she lost the little bit of money she had.

I sat her down and told her to be honest and find out what went wrong. The biggest mistake she made was not sticking to the stop loss – changing it because she had believed that she had made the correct call and the market would come back in her favour and the system was God. The other things are a bit more peripheral and come down to being in the right frame of mind. Firstly, when you go live and you use real money, whether you like it or not, your decision-making changes, causing a little bit of doubt and indecision. Her judgement was slightly clouded. Because of her illness she really wanted this to work so that she could stop doing her eight-hour a week job; her mind was in the wrong place. I also discovered she finds it hard to take failure, keeping her trades open rather than admitting she was wrong and cutting her losses. Too competitive!

I learned a lot from her and when I do my trading I try to be as dispassionate as possible. But hey, I'm only human! I have discovered that equally as important as research is having the correct head on. ❞

NT comments:

Exactly. You need to be unemotional when trading. Also, readers should beware of buying systems. The people selling them just want your money and I never heard of one that really works long term.

I broke the rules

Richard's tale:

" Now back at it after going back to the drawing board for three months!

Reason: I lost £1000 pounds in about four weeks, and yes I did everything it says not to do in your book *The Naked Trader*. I just can't seem to help myself.

Lowering the stop loss until I daren't any more, because I think I've got it.

Gosh, it looks so easy until you have money on it! Then you ask yourself, 'Is it a conspiracy?'

Anyway, here we go, a bit more learned than before...Oh crap, just stopped me out on AstraZeneca. **"**

NT comment:

Well it is what happens if you don't *trade your plan*. If you start lowering stop losses all the time and can't help yourself, you really have to consider whether spread betting is for you. Or it might be worth going flat then starting again.

Spread betting is no holiday

Peter's tale:

" I was really keen to have a go at spread betting for at least a couple of reasons. The first is no tax is payable. And that's always tempting!

The second reason is hindsight. Why? Yes, of course: *That company I had my eye on – look, it went up 5, 10, 20 points today. I just knew that was about to happen, but didn't buy it in time. And how much I've missed out!* I still find this happens a lot even now. The trouble is I only remember these moments, and don't notice the times when I held out from a stock and it went down.

So, with this rather breezy mindset, I launched forth into spreads. First, long some Glaxo. Made a nice £780 in two weeks. Whoops, lost £130 on Bradford & Bingley (remember them?), made £550 on BlueBay in a week, lost £90 on Nat Grid, then made £470 on Bradford again, and another £100 on Vislink. Lost another £105 with Alliance and Leicester, then made £140 with Barclays. So in the first month I made £2040 and lost £325: not bad.

Could I keep this up? Sure, why not?

Then I went skiing for a week, having set some stop losses up. Perhaps I didn't get them set right – too overconfident, the old downside blindspot kicking in again. The long and short of it is, I got stuffed with Alliance for £3000. The lesson for me here is to bloody well close everything out before going on holiday. I kept thinking about this while zipping down the slopes and not being able to get access to a screen and do anything about it.

Following that, on return I then had the house builders begin to tank. I was thinking they were always about to rebound and got stuffed again for £900 and then again for £2100. Old Mutual and Sage added nearly £550 and a rights issue with RBS added another £550, interspersed with about ten quite small losses. Then I felt I needed to give it all a rest, until I went on a 'Robbie' course.

However, since then I have done much better research and used much more discipline in picking shares. Once I had cleared out some old crap shares, the last 18 trades have seen 14 gains and four losses. I do have a bit more crap to clear out, but it seems to be going in the right direction. Once I get this going again, I may get back into spreads, but only perhaps three or four at most, since I find you have to think of these (like sex and money) all the time. And it also helps to be a little bit more worried now and then about the downside! **"**

NT comments:

Thanks Peter – I would say keeping spread bets open when on holiday without access to the net is dangerous. It might be worth closing out the really volatile ones before heading off. Also, early success is dangerous and can lead to overconfidence and too high stakes. Glad you are doing better now after my course!

Things I should have known

Hamish's tale:

" First, the reason why I spread bet. I did some trading (inspired by your books) but I've got quite a small portfolio (about £2k) and found that I was paying a fortune in commissions. Paying £20 or £30 on a £500 trade is quite a large percentage. With spread betting I can trade as I like but with very small amounts. I typically use between 50p and £3 a bet. Also, if I want, I can set guaranteed stops so I know exactly how much I'm risking.

Over time I'm gradually increasing my stakes as I build up my knowledge, and hopefully my pot. Most people say that you shouldn't do spread betting until you've mastered investing and trading, but I think in many ways it's actually easier for a novice.

Some really, really obvious things which I didn't realise at first:

- The actual level of the share price is a much bigger factor than in trading. Betting on a share at 800p which moves 10% risks a lot more than betting at 100p and moving 10%.

- Spread bets expire. A few days ago I was quite happily watching my market go up, only to realise that the bet had been closed the night before when it expired.

- Setting limits is good; it lets you catch unusual spikes either to get in or out.

- Planning bets when the market is closed really does help. **"**

NT comments:

Great points from Hamish. Always check the expiry date. And level of price is very important. Always know what your exposure is.

Beware Ye

Well, I hope you enjoyed those stories and learnt something from them all. Thank you to all of you who wrote them; it took some courage to admit what happened to you.

All the mistakes made in these stories, and the lessons they learned, are really valuable. It cost these readers many thousands of pounds to learn them, but only cost you the few quid you paid for this book. Bargain or what?

These tales are all true and all can be learned from. Worth keeping those stories by your bed and keep reading them – you may well either already, or soon, recognise yourself in one of them. If so, take heed of the warning!

12. Which Firm Should I Use?

As you can imagine, over the years I have probably used most of them! There are a large number of firms all offering different platforms and they're all good at different things.

I've personally, for now, narrowed it down to three firms that I regularly use – all three offer me something different. The great thing about spread betting and firms is that you don't really need to show any loyalty. It's not like a broker, where it's hard to move. You can sell up your positions if you don't like a firm and move somewhere else.

Also I believe it's worth having an account with more than one spread bet firm. Then, when it comes to placing a bet you can shop around. Who is offering a tighter spread on a particular bet you want to place? Who has best execution on certain bets? And who messes you about?

I tend to use Tradefair for FTSE trades and trades in the bigger shares. It has a one point daily FTSE spread which is excellent and I love the platform and the ease in dealing. I find trades usually get executed in a millisecond. It also puts on a stop loss for you, which is good discipline.

I use IG for trading the small companies – most spread firms, including Tradefair, don't allow you to spread bet the very small companies, but IG does. This is brilliant for me, as it enables me to trade the smaller AIM shares free of tax. IG also has an excellent charting pack, a decent platform and very good execution too.

Finally, I use Finspreads as my third company – sometimes it comes up with a better spread for me so I use it as my 'shopping around' firm. For new traders, for a while it offers the chance to spread bet at just 10p a point – a great way to get started without the risk of losing much.

I've also visited all three and I'm happy with the way customers are treated and that they are going with you and not against you.

I've also asked the three of them for some offers and you will find those at the end of the book – there are special links you can use there.

Of course, do your own research – and maybe visit some bulletin boards or ask around. Like me, after a while you will get used to one or two or three companies that you find you like over the others. Always search around before signing up, as some spread bet firms have bad reputations. I don't fancy being sued so can't tell you which ones here, but look around the boards for people complaining about specific companies!

In the end, of course, if you are not happy with the way a firm is treating you, just move onto another. There will always be plenty of competition. One final point is: if you have tons of capital, it's definitely worth keeping money with different firms. Because, in the unlikely event they go bust, the max you could get back under the current law is about £50,000.

13. The Rules

If you have the concentration span of a bored goldfish (...hmmm... now where was I again? Oh yes, writing this book) or just couldn't be arsed to read the whole book (I blame the parents) then fear not, because here's a rinky-dinky summary of the main points.

But first, some key advice...

Take it slow and steady

If there is one thing I'd like you to take away (curry and chips?) it's this –

Please. There is no need for you to rush into spread betting. Take your time. Do it slowly. Learn as much as you can about it and decide what kind of spread bettor you are and why you are doing it.

Also, take your time with trades. Let them develop a little; don't open and close them all the time.

And now, my 20 key rules for spread betting.

The Naked Trader Spread Betting Rules

1. Keep stakes to a level you can afford.

2. Don't use too much of the leverage offered.

3. A margin call could be a wake up call.

4. Stick to stop losses...

5.   ...but beware of the 8am stop-out and amend if necessary.

6.   Don't open too many positions.

7.   Beware fat fingers – check your trade before placing it.

8.   Don't get smug after winning and over-stake.

9.   Think mainly shorter-term trades...

10.   ...but longer-term ones can work too.

11.   Be careful trading volatile indices and commodities.

12.   Think about going short as well as long.

13.   Check ex-dividend and reporting dates.

14.   Cut losers quickly, and hang onto winners for more profit.

15.   Use resistance and support levels to help set stops and targets.

16.   Don't only rely on technical analysis.

17.   Beware tipsters and systems sellers.

18.   Be your own person – don't get influenced by others.

19.   Make sure you know what you are doing!

20.   Never tell your partner how much you are losing. (Kidding!)

Ultimately, it'll all slot into place and become quite simple with time: it really boils down to getting rid of any losses quickly and trying to hang onto the good winners for a bit, whether short or long.

That's a bit bloody obvious, you say?

Well, it should be now you've read this book. But upwards of 75% of spread bettors lose (and often lose badly) through the lack of a simple disciplined approach. More fool them.

Be severe with your losers and generous with your winners: the human brain is more often inclined to go the other way, and give extra time to duffers whilst nervously banking profits as soon as they appear.

Anyway that's my 40,000 words done. [Actually, Robbie, you wrote over 50,000. Once you start rabbitting... – Ed]

I do really hope this book helps, and that you find, over the years, that spread betting provides an excellent tool for your trading and investing. It *is* dangerous and most people lose. And you must be ready to accept that spread betting might not be for you. But for those who are determined to do it, do so safely, enjoy it, and – good luck!

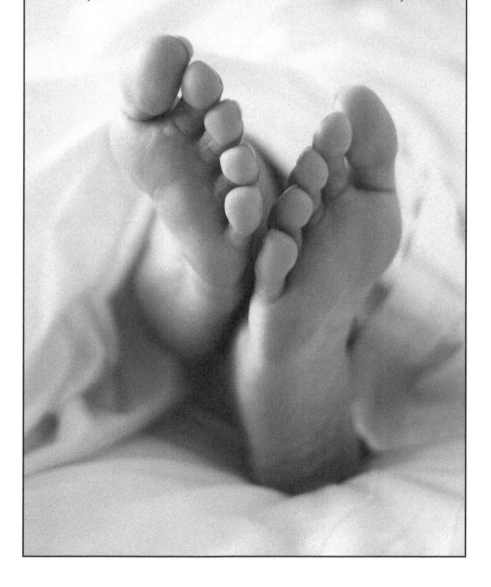

APPENDICES
(AKA Goodies at the End of the Book)

A few goodies hiding at the end of the book here.

I.   Jargon – we crunch some nasty terminology

II.   The Naked Trader Spread Betting Quiz – to test if you've been paying attention

III.   My website! – lots of fun

IV.   Naked Trader Seminars – even more fun

V.   Special Spread Betting Offers – some snazzy offers for book readers

There's only word for it: Whoo!

I. Jargon

Spread betting seems to contain quite a lot of jargon, which no one likes, so here is my guide to it. No need to freak out. Let's knock it all on the head for good. Boff!

Arbitrage

In the past occasionally two spread betting firms would have different prices for the same bet and one could take advantage by buying the bet with one SB firm and selling with another. Riskless money, but unusual these days.

Ask

The price you buy at. (Also called the *offer*.)

Bargain

Just means a trade. (Let's hope it becomes a bargain in due course.)

Bid

The price you sell at.

Bid-ask spread

The difference between the sell and buy price.

Binary bet

Fixed-odds betting provided by spread firms. Don't touch it, as you'll lose.

Cash call

The call you don't want from a spread firm asking you for, well, cash. Or more likely your debit card number...

Closing

Ending your bet to take a profit or loss.

Expiry

The date a bet expires.

GFD

Good For the Day – your order will be cancelled at the end of the day if it hasn't been executed.

GOG

Grumpy Old Git – what most spread bettors become! You'll find them on the bulletin boards.

GTC

Good Till Cancelled – your order will stay in the market till it is executed or you cancel it.

Leverage

Using borrowed money from the spread firm to trade.

Limit order

An order different from the current price. So if something is 100p to buy, you put in a limit order of 99p – your trade will only be triggered if that price is hit.

Long

A buy. Or betting on something to go up.

Margin/margin call

The amount you need in an account to order to open a position. If you run out of ready funds a margin call is the bookie calling and asking you for more readies. And you'd better have them or there will be trouble.

Market makers

The people that shift the prices up and down, causing you to lose money.

Notional trading requirement (NTR)

Boring term for the money you need in your account for a bet to be allowed to be opened. (This is also called *margin*.)

Offer

The price you buy at. (Also called the *ask*.)

Quarterly

A bet that expires at the end of the trading quarter – usually 4pm on the third Tuesday of March, June, September and December.

Rollover

Your bet in an expiring quarterly is closed and then reopened in the next quarterly the next day. On quarterlies the profit or loss is added or taken out of your account and you start again with the price for the next quarter. It costs a few quid to rollover, but the SB firms do give you a better spread to ease the pain.

Short

Betting on something to go down.

Stop loss

A fixed price where you ask the SB firm to close your bet at a loss for fear of losing more money.

Tick

The smallest movement possible in a share or index.

II. The Naked Trader Spread Betting Quiz

Huzzah! I've put the kettle on and fired up the toaster – as readers of my first book or website will know, two of the most important trading tools out there. It's quiz time with me at NT HQ.

1. *You get a call asking you for some margin. Do you reply:*

A. Oh, I'm the cleaner, can I take a message?

B. I'll send you the money right away.

C. I'll close out some positions to make us clear.

D. I am leaving the country – you will never find me.

2. *A bet price is close to your stop loss. Do you:*

A. Close it out, it wasn't right.

B. Buy some more to average down.

C. Lower the stop loss to give you more legroom.

D. Wonder what a stop loss is?

3. *Your partner spots on your computer that you are losing money spread betting. Do you:*

A. Admit it and have a talk about it.

B. Say: "Well, at least it wasn't porn."

C. Say you are winning really, that was just the loss for today.

D. Run off with a Slovakian pole-dancer.

4.   *You've got £5000 you can afford to lose. Do you:*

A.   Open loads of accounts to use the leverage.

B.   Only expose yourself to £5000 of shares.

C.   Use stop losses, so you can't lose more than £5000.

D.   Buy up £35,000 of stock using leverage to really go for it.

5.   *You see the FTSE falling fast. Do you:*

A.   Get on a short to follow the trend.

B.   Go long, it's about to bottom out.

C.   Leave it alone, go have a cup of tea.

D.   Short to hedge some share longs.

6.   *A friend says he is making a fortune trading forex. Do you:*

A.   Follow him eagerly into the next trade.

B.   Ask him his tactics and also buy some books on it.

C.   Ask him to admit what he's lost, too.

D.   Say well done then move onto another topic.

7.   *You see an ad for an amazing spread betting trading system. Do you:*

A.   Think you might buy it; it would save time if you're following a system.

B.   Buy the system. After all, look at the profits it's made already.

C.   Think there's one born every minute.

D.   See if you can invest in the company selling it.

8.   *You're making money spread betting. A friend asks if they can follow you. Do you:*

A.   Say, "Sure, I'll mail you all my trades."

B.   Teach them the nuts and bolts but tell them to make their own trades.

C.   Tell them to spend some time learning before trading.

D.   Divert them from the topic and start talking football.

Tea and Toast Note: The secret to great toast? *Don't burn it!* I used to own a café and had a great cook. Except she always burnt the toast; it used to drive me bananas. My favourite marmalade is Tesco's Finest, of which exquisite substance I get through about three jars a week. Yum.

---

9.   *Who of the below would make the best spread bettor?*

A.   Jordan

B.   Mr Spock [Surely Mr Stock? – Ed]

C.   Corporal Jones

D.   Lady Gaga

10.   *All your accounts are losing big-time. Do you:*

A.   Hide behind the sofa.

B.   Get a mate to bail you out.

C.   Close all positions, get out and pay up.

D.   Open another one up to try and win back losses.

11. *What is leverage?*

A.   A new track by Dizzee Rascal

B.   Money you're in effect borrowing from the spread firm.

C.   What you use to change a tyre.

D.   Money you put into your spread account.

12. *What is a rollover?*

A.   A bet that is closed then reopened for the next quarter.

B.   Something you do with your partner.

C.   What you did at school once in PE.

D.   A bet that gets renewed daily.

13. *A short-term trade keeps going up, past target. Do you:*

A.   Take profits immediately.

B.   Top slice some profit and leave the rest to run.

C.   Dance round the room in your undies singing *Halleluiah*.

D.   Keep the bet going longer-term to run the profit.

14. *You banked a massive win of £10,000 on a trade. Do you:*

A.   Take half of it out of your spread account and bank it.

B.   Buy some brand new positions using the money.

C.   Brag about it to the hot one at work you secretly fancy.

D.   Use the whole gain to get loads more leverage.

15. *The author of this book is:*

A.   Highly intelligent, clever and a genius.

B.   Overrated and a waste of space.

C.   A total buls***** like all other financial 'experts'.

D.   Way too handsome to be a finance writer.

Now check your answers and tally up your score.

1.   A = 0 B = 4 C = 2 D = 0

2.   A = 4 B = 0 C= 2 D = 0

3.   A = 4 B = 0 C = 1 D = 1

4.   A = 0 B = 4 C = 3 D = 0

5.   A = 3 B = 0 C = 4 D = 3

6.   A = 0 B = 3 C = 4 D = 3

7.   A = 0 B = 0 C = 4 D = 2

8.   A = 0 B = 3 C = 4 D = 3

9.   A = 0 B = 4 C = 0 D = 1

10.   A = 0 B = 0 C = 4 D = 0

11.   A = 0 B = 4 C = 0 D = 0

12.   A = 4 B = 0 C = 0 D = 4

13.   A = 1 B = 3 C = 0 D = 4

14.   A = 4 B = 0 C = 0 D = 0

15.   Anyone answering A or D gets two bonus points.

Over 45

Wow! Great score! I think you're going to do pretty well and you must have read the whole book and not skipped. Well done!

32-44

Not bad! You have some of the attributes needed to become a good spread bettor but might just need to do a little more reading up.

27-31

Just about got a chance, but you have a lot more work to do before opening an account. In particular, go back and check through the key things I've said, especially the basics.

27 and below

Bollocking time: on the naughty step, right now! You got a bad score and I even gave you a point for Lady Gaga! Don't think about spread betting until you have done a lot more reading up. But, in the end, maybe you're better suited to a flutter on the 4.20 at Kempton.

III. My Website!

You can catch up with my spread betting adventures at my website, www.nakedtrader.co.uk (currently updated twice a week). Unless you got this in the bargain bin in 2020, when I guess I might be doing other things. (Or maybe I met my maker: "Hi, hey before you judge me remember I gave that *Big Issue* guy £20...")

My email address is robbiethetrader@aol.com. I'm happy to answer emails but one thing I can't do is offer any advice as to whether you

should buy, sell or hold anything! Also, I do get a *lot* of mails so please be kind and stick to 150 words or less – no life stories! And do check the FAQs on my website, as the answer you could be seeking might already be there.

IV. Naked Trader Seminars

I hold five or six seminars a year, which are designed for beginners and improvers. Although spread betting is covered, including live trades on the day, the event is generally about how to make money on the markets, using different strategies, up or down. The whole day is live from the markets – indeed, I even usually place one or two spread bets live!

If you're interested in coming along and spending the day with me and the live markets and some interesting people email me (robbiethetrader@aol.com) with 'Seminars interested' in the subject line and I'll send you the info. It even includes a nice lunch! More information, including forthcoming seminar dates, can also be found on my website.

V. Special Spread Betting Offers

As mentioned elsewhere in the book, I use a number of spread bet firms and in the main I've ended up with the following three I like best – see the bit I wrote earlier in the book explaining why. I've asked each if they could make some kind of offer to readers and each has come up with a page that you can click on where you can sign up for the firm in question and pick up some freebie or other. Here they are as it stands – the offers may change as the book ages but hopefully if you try any of these links there should be something there for you!

- **IG Index** (Great for trading small cap shares). Offers readers a comprehensive charting package and 'TradeSense' – educational emails. www.igindex.co.uk/nakedtrader

- **Tradefair** (Tight spreads on the bigger companies and one point on the FTSE rolling). They're offering a £100 credit to your account. Plus you get a book of trading rules. www.tradefair.com/promo/spreads/nakedtrader100

- **Finspreads** offers just 10p a point on spread bets for a while, giving you the chance to test out spread betting with real money but low stakes. It also offers readers £100 credit. www.finspreads.com/nakedtrader

- **ADVFN** offers cheap Bronze (for Top Lists), cheap Silver (for real-time prices) and cheap Level II (for, erm, Level II) for my readers. Go to my website and mail me for details.

- Just to add, terms and conditions will apply with any of the offers so check the small print – i.e. to claim the credits you might have to make, say five trades first, etc.

There are tons of other spread-bet firms, have a Google! You may find some other offers at my website www.nakedtrader.co.uk as well as my twice weekly blog. Catch you there!

Index

"Read. Read. And read some more."

— The Naked Trader
(2nd edition)

Top Trading and Investment Titles from

Harriman House

The Naked Trader (2nd edition)
How anyone can make money trading shares
Robbie Burns
9781905641512

The Financial Spread Betting Handbook
A guide to making money trading spread bets
Malcolm Pryor
9781897597934

Entry Level Spread Betting Strategies (DVD)
Winning techniques for traders
Malcolm Pryor
9780857190383

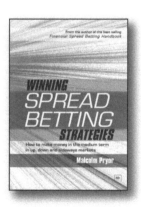

Winning Spread Betting Strategies
How to make money in the medium term in up, down and sideways markets
Malcolm Pryor
9781906659103

Spread Betting the Forex Markets
An expert guide to spread betting the foreign exchange markets
David Jones
9781906659516

The Investor's Toolbox
How to use spread betting, CFDs, options, warrants and trackers to boost returns and reduce risk
Peter Temple
9781905641048

Hh | Harriman House

Top Trading and Investment Titles from

Harriman House

The Zulu Principle
*Making extraordinary
profits from ordinary shares*
Jim Slater
9781905641918

**The Street-Smart
Trader**
*An insider's guide to the
City*
Ian Lyall
9781906659073

**High Performance
Trading**
*35 Practical Strategies and
Techniques to Enhance
Your Trading Psychology
and Performance*
Steve Ward
9781905641611

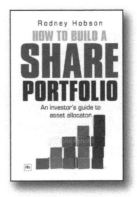

**Understanding
Company News**
*How to interpret stock
market announcements*
Rodney Hobson
9781906659226

**The   Commodities
Investor**
*A beginner's guide to
diversifying your portfolio
with commodities*
Philip Scott
9781905641833

**How to Build a
Share Portfolio**
*An investor's guide to asset
allocation*
Rodney Hobson
9780857190215

Hh   Harriman House